W9-CYZ-723

OUR REBEL EMOTIONS

OUR REBEL EMOTIONS

by

Bernard Mobbs

THE SEABURY PRESS
New York

To Brenda

CONTENTS

Foreword

FOREWORD
by the Rev. Canon J.B. Phillips, D.D.

Among my many friends and acquaintances I can think of a number to whom this short book would be quite valueless. Indeed, some of them would be incapable of imagining why it should be written. These are healthy extroverts who have no knowledge whatever of the assorted hells which can make an attack, and sometimes a very prolonged attack, upon those who suffer from a condition which is still popularly called 'nerves'. It is useless to try and make them see, good and kind people though they may be, anything of the terrifying and apparently unending darkness through which thousands of their fellow-men are having to pass. It is like trying to explain the beauties of a picture to the blind or the subtleties of harmony to the totally deaf.

But I also know both in my own person and through the evidence of a heavy correspondence, that a great many people are alarmed and disturbed by the outward manifestations of their own 'rebel emotions'. Part of their horror, and in some cases despair, lies in the fact that although they can hear the distant battle- cries and experience in a hundred different ways the mental pain and the exhaustion produced by these battles, they have no idea what they are all about. What makes matters even worse, if they are trying to follow the Christian way, is that the sense of God disappears, their faith wavers and the habit of prayer, which had previously helped them, now seems useless and irrelevant. Some, though by no means all, are lucky enough to be cured quite rapidly through recently-discovered drugs, and others by wise psychiatrists. But I become more and more convinced that there is a large anonymous body of men and women who stoically endure until even hope itself is almost extinguished. The burden is in no way relieved by those who tell them to 'pull themselves together'; and, since they are usually conscientious and responsible people, they blame themselves for their condition and the burden of guilt is added to their physical symptoms and mental pain.

I think that this book, although by itself unlikely to effect a cure, may prove the beginning of a way out from an intolerable situation. The very fact that it is written by a non-professional with no axe to grind and no rigid systems or theory into which all human beings may be conveniently classified makes it particularly helpful. I would not claim to know Major Bernard Mobbs very well, but I am perfectly certain that no one could write a book half as good as this unless he himself had known irrational fears and felt black despondency. 'He jests at scars that never felt a wound' and it is only those who have themselves been wounded in spirit who can appreciate the sense of failure and utter futility which are the lot of those for whom the light and colour have gone out of the business of living. The writer is plainly concerned most of all to show some light in the dark and frightening places.

The book also interests me because it shows the part of real Christianity as opposed to 'religion' in setting the wounded spirit on the road to recovery. The author makes no wild or extravagant claims, and he is scrupulously fair to the psychiatrists who regard 'religion' as a serious barrier to the patient's growth into an integrated human being. But he believes, as I do myself, that the whole business of self-knowledge and the recovery of self-confidence is very closely connected with a right and proper view of God as revealed to us in Christ. There are certain things about us which can never, and probably should never, be changed. We are no more responsible for them than we are for our own heredity. But in this book we are shown how drives and emotions, which frighten us by their violence and apparent evil, can be transformed in the process of making a man into an integrated personality instead of a human being who is not much more than a mobile civil war.

I think Major Bernard Mobbs is particularly wise in his

words about the difference between what is commonly called morality, which can be a strait-jacket to the personality, and the way of love taught and demonstrated by Jesus. We can see far more clearly why the bitterest enemies of Jesus in His earthly life were not the 'baddies' but the 'goodies'! He repeats this in slightly varying terms but it is well worth repeating. For many of those who would call themselves Christians find it difficult to think of the Christian way of life as anything other than a kind of bargain made with the Almighty, whereby if we are 'good' He treats us well and if we are 'bad' He will painfully correct us. The idea that God really is Love, and really does love us whatever we are or whatever we do, is an extremely difficult idea for the human spirit to grasp. We cannot be relieved of self-hatred and self-contempt until we know something of God's love for us *as we are*. And until we have recovered a normal and proper love for ourselves, our love for other people remains a spiritual chore.

Many years ago a very eminent and widely experienced psychiatrist (who, alas, has been dead for some time) said to me, 'If the neurotic (by which he meant all those who are emotionally disturbed) could only see the love of God, he might well be instantaneously cured.' He said this with a rather wry smile since the neurotic, partly through his own illness, has a very distorted idea of the love of God. But I believe it to be essentially true, and thus I am not in the least surprised that when the love of God was focussed in a perfect human being, in Jesus Christ, we read again and again that He 'cast out devils'. This may well be the language of 2,000 years ago, but those who have suffered the torments will hardly think that 'the devils' are an exaggeration. Today, however, the mediators of God's love, 'the casters-out of devils', must be human beings, who are themselves imperfect. And there is a desperate shortage of men and women with compassion, who know enough and care enough to be such mediators. Again and again the author of this book points out the need for the church to be a true fellowship where healing can begin. Among its members there should be some who can be 'counsellor', 'confessor', 'director' or simply good honest trustworthy friend, through whom the process of re-adjustment to ourselves as we are and life as it is may be made. There are some who can make this progress through direct intercourse with God, but the author, who is always realistic, admits that they are few. For most people the acceptance of our 'rebel emotions' and their re-direction into constructive paths can only be through the help of a wise and trusted friend. The author wisely points out that there are some 'maladjusted personalities' who can only be helped by those specially trained to deal with the alarming outward signs of a deep inner conflict.

I have great pleasure, then, in recommending this book for its wisdom, patience and compassion. It is scrupulously honest, down-to-earth and never tries to minimise the difficulties which lie in the path to recovery. It is plainly based on observation of real life and on experience of the agonies which conflicting emotions can produce. It should bring hope to many who are baffled or deeply ashamed of what goes on within themselves. It should also prove valuable to the pastor who has no technical training but is nonetheless prepared to pay the price in patience and in giving time and encouragement to those who seek his help.

'These horrid feelings'

CHAPTER 1

'These horrid feelings'

'Don't ask me to add Christianity to all my other burdens.' This was the plea of a distressed woman who suspected that her counsellor was about to introduce a religious note into their conversation. Her honest protest echoes the sentiments of many who have to battle against disabling anxieties, humiliating fears and bewildering moodiness. One reason why Christian faith is seen by such people as an added burden, rather than increased resources, is that they imagine a Christian is expected to have perfect control over an area of his personality which is mostly beyond conscious control—his emotions. A Christian, they imagine, must always *feel* tranquil, loving, trustful and chaste.

This assumption is also shared by many Christians who are too loyal to describe their religion as an added burden. That their faith does not automatically release them from emotional conflict should be no cause for alarm. It could be argued that religion no more exempts a person from being emotionally maimed or wounded than it makes him accident proof. What is profoundly disturbing is to find that so many Christians who suffer more or less severe forms of nervous illness, far from being enabled by their faith to wrest some gains from the experience, only feel more guilty and more wretched than if they were unbelievers.

This book is primarily addressed to those suffering from depression, anxiety and other emotional disturbances. Indeed, to all those whose 'rebel emotions' at times make them miserable and rob them of a full life. Just how much suffering is involved in emotional disorder has to be

13

experienced or observed at close quarters to be believed. Even quite serious physical illnesses can often be cured by surgery or intensive medical care. Yet while great strides are being made in psychiatry, it is still true that many nervous sufferers endure years of mental anguish. There is a vast company of people who are not ill enough to quality for a place on the over-crowded waiting lists for psychiatric help; yet are too disturbed to enjoy life as they otherwise could.

This book is written in the belief that a Christian can find resources in his faith which will help him to endure mental pain creatively. What is often called a 'nervous breakdown' can be an opportunity for new growth and development. A 'breakdown' can sometimes be transformed into a breakthrough. It is good for some of us that the personality structure we have erected over the years, the foundations of which were laid long before we were capable of playing a conscious part, has proved inadequate. Indeed, the greatest danger is that we may merely try to repair the rents and resume life where we left off, that our 'breakdown' may pass without our gaining the kind of insight that leads to change.

In asking what resources the Christian faith has to offer to those with emotional problems we shall inevitably have to deal with the broader issue of how it assists and facilitates the growth of the personality. For most neurotic suffering arises precisely because there has been some failure to become emotionally adult. It is possible, for instance, to grow up physically and not outgrow the dependency of childhood. The very intensity of the suffering involved is an indication of the struggle going on in the depths to overcome resistances to growth.

Furthermore, it is being increasingly realised that full maturity is a goal most of us have yet to reach. Rather than label people as 'neurotic' it is better to talk about neurotic reactions or neurotic traits, for few of us are entirely free from these. 'We all have neurotic symptoms', writes Anthony Storr, a psychoanalyst. 'The better one gets to know both one's friends and oneself, the more one can see in operation the identical defence mechanisms, neurotic character traits and periodic symptoms which are presented in the course of analysis by a patient on the couch.'

To enquire, then, into what should be the Christian's attitude to his 'rebel emotions' is at the same time to ask what kinds of religious practice encourage personal development.

* * *

We should be clear at the start that nobody was ever cured of depression, or resolved their deep-seated conflicts, only by reading a book. The problem of writing for the sufferer from 'nerves' is that advice which may bring real alleviation to one person may prove quite impracticable to another. For instance, many have found relief from nervous tension through the sustained practice of muscular relaxation. Yet another person's anxieties may be so acute that relaxation is not only impossible, but the attempt to achieve it without any other assistance only increases his distress.

What can be written which would prove helpful, even in varying degrees, to the young person who is too painfully shy to enter a restaurant or go to a party, the woman who spends the first half of every day under a blanket of depression, the man who vainly battles with a host of grotesque sexual fantasies or the church worker who must live in a whirl of activity in order to keep at bay a pack of crouching anxieties? Any personal counsellor is so aware of the diversity of emotional problems that he would surely refuse to go into print but for one important fact. The number of disturbed and troubled people who receive skilled counselling, or psychiatric help, is infinitesimal compared with those who struggle on without it, either because they cannot bring themselves to share their problem or because, for the comparatively minor disability they suffer, no skilled help is available. A book cannot substitute for a good personal counsellor, but a book may sometimes give enough insight to modify our problems for the better.

Furthermore, by giving some understanding of how emotional disorders arise we can hope to ease the painful bewilderment of those who accuse themselves, and are sometimes accused by their acquaintances, of weakness or worse. Depression and anxiety are not caused by our own mismanagement of our lives: they are often related to factors in our early environment for which neither we, nor often our parents, were responsible. Recognising the links between our childhood and our present problems at least lessens our perplexity, even when it does not remove our symptoms.

A book may also try to show how a Christian may bring his mental pain within the orbit of his religious faith, rather than regarding it as something wholly alien, something which just ought not to be. We are ready to admit that some of the greatest saints have been people who endured physical suffering creatively. 'I thank God for my handicaps', wrote Helen Keller after years of blindness and deafness, 'for through them I have found myself, my work and my God.' Is there no way of facing up to our fears and anxieties so they too may bring us nearer to God and better equip us to help our fellows? How shall we practise our faith so that it may, if possible, assist our healing, and will in any case lead towards greater maturity and growth?

It is to the answering of these questions that this book is particularly addressed. For everyone who has any experience in helping troubled souls will confirm that in all too many instances religion is misunderstood in a way which increases inferiority, aggravates anxiety and blocks self-understanding. The hostility of some psychiatrists towards religion arises in part because they fear how damaging its misapplication could be to some of their patients. Yet many more would agree that the Christian gospel, properly appreciated, is powerfully therapeutic.

16

Jesus invited all who were weary and over-burdened to come to Him for rest of soul (Matthew 11:28-30). His offer was not to the well-balanced, perfectly adjusted individuals, if such existed, who found no difficulty in coping with life. While it is no more true to claim that religious belief saves a person from emotional conflict than to assert it always prevents physical disability, we cannot make the opposite assumption that faith has absolutely nothing to do with this area of life. Every personal counsellor could record instances where religious faith has been the decisive element either in the resolution of inner conflict or in yielding courage to endure with dignity, and make positive use of, suffering. Similarly, it is by no means rare that the greatest hindrance on the way to healing is a distorted view of God or a harshly negative morality. If religion is not a cure-all, neither is it irrelevant, and it is to the understanding of its relationship to these problems that we will later turn.

*   *   *

Our 'rebel emotions' are not feelings we should utterly disown, if we could, for the rest of our lives. Under certain conditions it is right and healthy to feel strongly the whole range of human emotion. If we cannot be angry at the sight of gross injustice, temporarily depressed at the failure of a good cause, anxious when a dear one's health is threatened, sexually aroused by the embrace of a beloved partner, then we are maimed personalities. And there are good grounds for believing that in such 'unemotional' personalities feeling is not really lost, but driven underground.

Strong emotions are not to be regretted or repressed. The problem for so many is that their emotions are misplaced and unconnected with their environment. They reflect, not their actual situation, but what is going on at a deep unconscious level of their personalities. So on a bright spring day, when work is going well and our family circle provides us with all the loving security we could wish for, we become unaccountably depressed. Or a situation in which there is only the barest minimum of danger, like crossing a road, becomes an ordeal for which we have to gather together the last ounce of our courage, or capitulate in humiliation to nameless dread. The relative or colleague who, at worst, should provoke us to occasional irritation and annoyance becomes the focus for a hatred which drives us to despair. It is in such situations that emotion, which should enrich our experience and empower our will, becomes a rebel. Our feelings are appropriate neither to our environment, nor to the ideals and goals we consciously cherish.

Our first reaction is to try to suppress these undesirable feelings, even to scold ourselves for having them. Sometimes we may succeed, though it would be a thousand pities to banish these rebels from consciousness without trying to learn from them a little more of the truth about ourselves. More often we fail and there ensues a long, exhausting battle between the feelings which refuse to be disowned and the 'self' which cannot see how such apparently destructive emotions can be integrated into the personality.

Faced with this conflict, we should first remind ourselves that emotional turmoil is potentially more hopeful than complete loss of feeling. We may envy the rather austere, highly-controlled person, who appears incapable of anger, grief or enthusiasm. Compared with our embattled personality he may seem all tranquility and peace. But if, too early in life to realise what he was doing, he had to cut himself off from his feelings, he has more problems than we have. At best, his rigidity limits his usefulness. At worst, a personal crisis may destroy his defences with bewildering results.

E.N. Ducker tells the story of a young man, very sick, who came to him for help. He had been an infant prodigy, able to carry on a conversation at the age of two and a master of the multiplication tables at four. His mother, supported by his father, trained her son solely by reasoned argument. The development of intuition and emotion was entirely neglected. Later, as a young adult, decisions which most people would make smoothly, intuitively and with a minimum of stress, involved him in endless calculations. He devised an intricate series of logical tests, requiring at least three months to complete, to assess the suitability of any particular girl whom he might wish to make his wife. Yet to try and live by the intellect alone is at last to reach an impasse, and so it was with this man.

Even that condition in which our feelings seem most useless, depression, is not entirely negative. When we are depressed we seem to have no feelings at all, except cold despair. Yet if, as has been claimed, depression is 'frozen passion' then we are here faced with a rebel who might conceivably be converted into an ally.

We need to take another look at those emotions which so distress us that we would eagerly sign on the dotted line for some kind of psychic amputation if only we could be rid of them. In their present form they certainly are enemies of our peace, but they need not remain so. Indeed, the trouble they now give us may be the measure of the neglect we have afforded them in the past.

When we have lost touch with our feelings and instincts or have become alienated from them, we should begin to regard them, says Gilbert Russell, as a father does his children. Most of his day is passed at the office or business, 'but unless he spends some part of it in the nursery he will lose all touch with his family, and the children become increasingly ill-at-ease, unhappy, rebellious, starved of love and the precious security of knowing themselves to be loved. A man who is cut off from the instinctual and emotional roots of his being might do worse than think of them as his neglected and anxious children, and of the renewal of the relationship as the act which, more than anything else, will bring fresh life and hope to himself and them.' How often a disturbed person will refer to 'these horrid feelings'! A lasting solution requires a more positive appreciation of our emotional endowment.

How shall we convert the rebels into allies? How can the delinquent children take their place again in a harmonious family circle? Is such an ideally happy outcome *always* possible?

To this last question we have, in all honesty, to answer: No. Yet short of a complete resolution of emotional conflicts a great deal can be achieved which lessens distress and prevents a problem from developing into total breakdown and disruption.

It has been a cardinal principle of most schools of psychotherapy that, as far as possible, we should try to trace the origins of present emotional distress back to our earlier life. This is not a cowardly evasion of responsibility: it is simply an honest recognition of the way human personality grows, with a view to taking appropriate action in the present. So, to take a few simple illustrations, we might come to see that our extreme touchiness toward our boss, and toward all authority figures, stems from our early experience with a domineering father. Or our fear of open spaces results from an over-protective and anxious mothering so that all excursions into the 'unknown' are even now felt to be fraught with danger. The guilty fascination which sexuality exercises in our thinking may be seen to be the outcome of an early inculcation of a 'puritan' suspicion of the body.

With comparatively mild disorders of the emotions this kind of insight can result in dramatic change. But even when the roots of our problems are too deeply buried for us to discover them unaided, or even when skilled help fails to make the necessary links, a tremendous relief comes with the recognition that our present distress has rational causes. We are depressed, anxious, obsessed, not because we are exceptionally ungrateful, selfish, or evil people, but because we have suffered psychic wounds which are as real and lasting as physical injury. Though this may not completely remove

20

our symptoms, it does liberate us from false guilt and remove the sheer bewilderment that merely increases our mental pain.

For this reason, we shall look in turn at some of the more common personality problems and seek to understand how they originate. Valuable as this is, however, it is not enough. Therapists who spend most of their time leading their patients towards such insights acknowledge that more is needed. Carl Jung describes a young man who came to him with a complete case history of his own neurosis. Jung could fault neither the man's historical reconstruction of his disorder, nor his understanding of his present condition. Yet the patient remained uncured.

Something more than insight is needed, and often it is in the realm of this 'something more' that a vital religious faith plays a part. As well as trying to understand the source of our conflicts we shall also ask what is the most appropriate response a Christian can make to them.

Depression—

   man against himself

CHAPTER 2

Depression—

man against himself

The Slough of Despond claims all of us at some time or another, but while many merely stumble around in its shallows there are some who sink into its foul depths to the point where life itself becomes a burden. Of first importance in dealing with depression, our own or another person's, is to recognise the difference between passing despondency, for which there may well be a good cause, and a depressive illness. This is not too difficult and, in any case, where there is any doubt at all, a doctor should be consulted.

The Greek philosopher Hippocrates, who lived four hundred years before Christ, made a fourfold classification of temperament: the impassive and somewhat lethargic he called *phlegmatic*—the passionate and ardent *choleric*—the buoyant and optimistic *sanguine*—the sober and somewhat gloomy *melancholic*. These categories have been replaced in modern studies of human personality but perhaps we can easily classify ourselves and some of our friends in this way.

If we are prone to low spirits which stop short of true depression we can usually develop techniques which at least enable us to limit the effects of our moods. We recognise, for instance, that judgment is inevitably impaired by a fit of the blues and refuse to make important decisions, or undertake tricky encounters, while the mood lasts. The old adage, 'Never get out of a train while it is standing in a tunnel', has saved many a despondent person from taking a step—such as resigning a post or emigrating to another country—he would later have regretted.

Most of us can recall occasions when we were lifted out of our despondency by trying to help another person. The dark clouds of gloom tend to thicken in isolation and disperse in the kind of company which helps us to forget ourselves. H.E. Fosdick pointed out the solitary nature of the mood we sometimes describe as 'sulky'. 'A sulky is a horse-drawn vehicle, consisting of a single seat on two wheels. The driver sits alone; no man can ride with him; he is essentially a solitary egoist. By a happy stroke of etymological common sense, "sulky" interprets the real meaning of "sulkiness".'

We can usually do something to lift ourselves out of despondency or a fit of sulks. This is less true of even a mild depression, and to tell a deeply depressed person to 'pull himself together' can be terribly dangerous.

Some doctors distinguish between depression which is triggered off by adverse circumstances such as bereavement, loss of work or strained relationships (reactive depression), and those depressions which appear quite unrelated to external circumstances (endogenous depression).

Depression may be entirely psychological, with little or no interference of bodily functions. Other depressions have marked adverse effect upon sleep, appetite, digestion, body temperature and weight, sexual potency and the menstrual cycle.

Recent years have witnessed vast advances in the treatment of depressive illness, and a huge burden of human suffering has been lifted from the shoulders of many sufferers by anti-depressant drugs and other physical treatments. Sometimes a course of such drugs is all that is necessary and, in any case, once depression has reached a certain depth, they will be needed to enable the patient to co-operate with the kind of psychotherapy which seeks to lay bare the causes of depression.

What are the causes? Has anything been learnt in treating the severe forms of this illness which may help us to understand our milder depressions?

It is an axiom with nearly all schools of psychotherapy that depression masks a deep-seated rage and anger. This is by no means apparent to the casual observer or even to the sufferer. The depressed person seems to lack enough energy to be really angry. Yet it is noticeable that an outburst of temper will often temporarily relieve depression, and such outbursts are taken as a sign of improvement by those who nurse depressed patients.

Sigmund Freud noticed that in his depressed patients the accusations and anger which they might with good reason have hurled against their environment, they in fact directed against themselves. He concluded that depression was rage turned inwards, anger diverted from its natural object towards the self. Since all this goes on beneath the level of consciousness the depressed person is the last in the world to admit that he feels angry. If he were more conscious of his anger he would be correspondingly less depressed.

Frank Lake, a Christian psychiatrist and founder of the Clinical Theology Association, has collected a number of quotations from early theological writers which indicate that they too recognised the link between anger and depression, which they called 'accidie'. 'This sadness', wrote the Shepherd of Hermas, 'is the sister of half-heartedness and bitterness.' 'Those who are sad after this fashion have anger already close to them', claimed Gregory the Great. And Dante distinguished the active wrath which vents itself on the exterior world, from the passive and sullen wrath leading to withdrawal and sadness.

To understand how a person can unconsciously direct rage and aggression against himself we need to go back to the first years of life. Many observers, and nearly all mothers, have commented at some time upon the intensity of a baby's anger when deprived or frustrated.

There is a great deal of evidence from psychiatrists and analysts to confirm the suspicion that babies react to being deprived of their mothers' loving presence in ways which can be terribly frightening to themselves. Mounting anxiety leads them either to pretend she is present or to rage at her absence. In either case fantasy, which is our earliest mode of thought, comes to their aid. The warm, full breasts are present in imagination, the child's own thumb sucked in place of the absent nipple. But there may also be a far more active, angry reaction in which the fantasies will be those of attack and aggression against the mother who is failing him in his moment of need. Yet these angry fantasies become terribly frightening for they envisage the destruction of the very thing upon which his life depends. They are therefore diverted from their true object and turned back upon the self.

Since young babies appear to be insatiable in their desire for attention it is inevitable that they all suffer frustration and have some difficulties in coping with consequent emotions. It is also true that many suffer more frustration than they ought to and so become more seriously stressed. The child who had much to be angry about and who was constitutionally predisposed to deal with his anger in this way will become a potential depressive, for throughout life he will be afraid of his own anger. He will attack himself rather than other people. Indeed, he will defend against the aggression he has buried by becoming over-compliant.

Winston Churchill waged a life-long battle against depression, which he called his 'Black Dog'. Although born into a wealthy and influential family there is ample evidence that his parents failed to give him the attention and affection that most children receive. They delegated their responsibilities to a 'nanny' while they themselves were fully occupied in social activities. Churchill's father showed little interest in and sometimes a considerable disapproval of his son, the boy who worshipped his father.

In his essay upon Winston Churchill in *Four Faces and the Man*, Anthony Storr writes, 'Psychiatrists have often observed that delinquent and emotionally disturbed children, who have parents who are actually neglectful or cruel, still maintain that these "bad" parents are really "good" and blame themselves for the parents' faults . . . Winston Churchill showed this idealisation very clearly. Of his mother, he wrote: "She shone for me like the evening star. I loved her dearly—but at a distance".' Concerning Churchill's attitude to his father, Violet Bonham Carter wrote: 'The image remained upon its pedestal, intact and glorious. Until the end he worshipped at the altar of his unknown father.'

Anthony Storr points out that the one period in Churchill's life when he had little difficulty in coping with his 'Black Dog' was when, during the second world war, his aggression and hostility could all be directed outwards towards the evil tyranny of Hitler's regime.

Children whose experience during the first years of their lives made them terrified of their own anger, so destructive did it seem of the very source of their life, may well find much in their later environment to confirm this fear and increase their repressions. This is particularly so in families which place an embargo on the expression of strong feelings.

Healthy human relationships contain negative as well as positive elements. A husband can become very annoyed with the wife he truly loves, but his affection is strong enough to contain such passing emotions. There are some families, however, where this reality is never faced. In these circles a 'good' relationship is one which is all sweetness and light, where hostility, frustration and irritation are never even felt, let alone expressed. Reared in such an unreal atmosphere a child becomes increasingly alienated from his own feelings of aggression. If his parents never express their negative emotions he is not free to express his. Yet the hostility does not thereby cease to exist. Driven underground, it is merely turned back upon himself. The child blames himself for having such wicked feelings.

One psychotherapist instituted in his family a period

which he called 'psychic toilet' when every member was expected to express his complaints about the conduct of the others. In this way hidden resentments were cleansed, dishonest pretence was banished and the need for repression was removed.

There is a great deal of psychological wisdom in William Blake's lines:

> I was angry with my friend,
> I told my wrath, my wrath did end.
> I was angry with my foe,
> I told it not, my wrath did grow.

There are good grounds for believing that the depressive is one who, for a variety of reasons, never learned how to 'tell his wrath'.

If this pattern of reaction is established early in life so that we direct our anger inwards instead of outwards it will obviously affect our religious life profoundly. Luther's confessor told him that he was angry with God, and this is a common cause of disorder in the religious life. God is supremely the One against whom a man may well fear to vent his wrath, yet life is such that angry questions sometimes rise to the lips of the most pious believer. That is, unless he is a typical depressive. In which case the anger will be cut off from consciousness but will continue to rage in the depths of the mind, giving rise to a depression. When our relationship with God is one of fear our religion perpetuates our depression rather than bringing the relief it otherwise could.

* * *

It might well be objected at this point that even if this view of the origin of depression is true, it is of little help. If the process by which rage and aggression is turned against ourselves early becomes an unconscious one what can we do about it?

This will largely depend upon the depth of the problem. In any case, what we may hope to achieve, as with all these difficulties, is never a miraculous and instantaneous cure, but rather a gradual growth in self-awareness with a consequent modification of our conflicts. Psychological perfection is as illusive as any other kind of perfection and not to be obtained in this world.

We can begin by asking ourselves whether there were factors in our early environment which inhibited the natural expression of anger, irritation and aggression. Naturally we cannot recall the babyhood experience of destructive rage which is sometimes the first stage in the formation of a depressive personality. But we do know whether our family background was one in which a healthy acceptance of negative emotions was possible.

It will also help if we can re-educate ourselves towards a more mature view of what constitutes a healthy human relationship. The danger of relationships in which negative feelings cannot be expressed is not merely that anger and irritation are directed elsewhere, perhaps against the family pet, more likely against ourselves in depression; but rather that when negative emotions are repressed so are positive ones. The person who is afraid of his emotions ends up by burying the good ones along with the bad. The result, in terms of our relationships, is a cold indifference.

Deeply repressed antagonisms and hatred do not surface from the depths of the mind just by making an act of will. It may well be that we need a wise friend or counsellor to help us face our negative emotions. We may be able to come to terms with them a little at a time as we relinquish our unrealistic view of what it means to be a human being and as we become less fearful of our own aggression.

* * *

Has the Christian any specific resources for coping with depression? Assuming that the above account of the causes of depression is correct, it is obvious that the depressive has two needs. If possible, he must recognise and come to terms with his own deep aggression and anger. Secondly, because ideal solutions are rare in these matters, he needs courage and faith to hold on during dark periods which continue to recur despite the medical treatment he may be receiving or the advances in self-awareness he has achieved.

Coming to terms with hidden anger and aggression will be more difficult for the Christian if he is burdened with a punitive image of God modelled upon those very parental figures who, with the best will in the world, first compelled him to repress his anger. God is not shocked by our rage, nor is it hidden from him even when we refuse to face it ourselves. If truth is to be the foundation upon which we build our personalities it is better that we learn to stand naked in the divine presence.

In his book *In Search of Maturity*, Fritz Kunkel describes the kind of prayer in which, before God, we can uncover and so come to terms with some of our early antagonisms. He advises us to go back in imagination to some of the earliest scenes of our lives. 'Be a child once more', he writes, 'frightened to death by your father's severity, or spoiled by the sentimentality of your aunt. And at the same time be there as the adult you are . . . Feel the child's anguish and fear, or, when spoiled, his shallow smugness. At the same time the adult's resentment will rise in angry waves. You will realise an anger, unknown so far, because it was carefully repressed. Now be honest. Tell your father or your aunt who are there without being there how you feel. They have poisoned your life, murdered your creativity. The terrific power of revenge will surge up from the unconscious and flood your consciousness. You may be carried away by your "sacred wrath"; but remember, God is still there, too.'

Kunkel goes on to point out that this exercise is no mere

self-justification, nor simply a discharge of personal vindictiveness. Waiting with your father or your aunt before God's tribunal you come to realise that 'you are certainly as weak and blind as your aunt or your father have been. You are also human, obsessed by the same collective images, caught in the same collective misery. So you may shake hands and forgive one another.'

This is very much the description of an ideal solution which is beyond the reach of most of us. Yet it is in this direction we should seek to move. Surely if there is any place on earth where we can admit and come to terms with our negative emotions it is in the presence of a God who knows all about us and loves us just the same.

Some of our repressed anger and resentment may be directed, not at parents and other important figures in our early life, but at God Himself. It is significant that many of the psalmists and other Biblical writers felt free to challenge God in a way that seems highly impious to our modern sensibilities. 'Wilt Thou be to me like a deceitful brook, like waters that fail?' asks Jeremiah. It is reported that Teresa of Avila once said to God, 'It is no wonder You have so few friends if You treat them all in this way.' When a relationship is deeply loving such honesty is possible. Is it because our relationship to God is less real that we assume such a guarded manner in His presence? Certainly such superficiality does not enable us to come to terms with our true selves.

The Cross of Christ offers deep resources to the depressed. For one thing we see there that God willingly exposes Himself to the wrath of man without any diminution of His love. There is a deeply moving scene in Peter de Vries' novel *The Blood of the Lamb* in which the hero, whose daughter has just died of leukaemia on her twelfth birthday, finds himself outside a church. He looks up at a crucifix and suddenly all his pent-up rage explodes. He takes a birthday cake which was to have been a part of the birthday celebrations at the hospital and hurls it at the face of the Man on the Cross. It lands squarely just beneath the crown of thorns. Then, in imagination, and through scalded eyes, he sees the fingers free themselves from the nails and move slowly to the soiled face. 'Very slowly, very deliberately, with infinite patience, the icing was wiped from the eyes and flung away.'

The saving truth of Calvary is that God positively invites us to vent our rage and anger upon Him, not that we may remain forever in a state of childish peevishness, but that we may come to terms with our hostility because we have discovered a love that is stronger than our hatred.

So Archbishop Leighton, writing in the seventeenth century to a depressed woman, advised: 'As a father pities his child when it is sick, and in the rage and reveries of a fever, though it even utter reproachful words against himself, shall not even our dearest Father both forgive and pity those thoughts in any child of His, that arise not from any wilful hatred of Him, but are kindled in hell within them? . . . In the meantime, when these assaults come thickest and violentest upon you, throw yourself down at His footstool and say, "O God, Father of mercies, save me from this hell within me" . . . Thus, or in whatever frame your soul shall be carried, to vent itself into His bosom.'

Even when we have consciously accepted this truth about God our anger may be too deep-seated to surface, and we remain depressed. It is then that the story of the Cross may yield another kind of strength, the strength to hold on in the dark. From the gospel records it is clear that this is just what Christ had to do.

Many devout Christians have suffered long periods of spiritual darkness. Professor John Baillie tells us that his brother, the well-known scholar and saint, Donald Baillie, had his spells of dejection and doubt. 'He was a martyr to a long-standing asthmatic condition, and the depression was physical as well as mental. He would put to himself and to me the question as to whether the extreme bodily lassitude was the cause, or the result, or merely the accompaniment, of the darkness of his soul.' He quotes his brother as saying to him on one occasion, 'When the darkness is on me I walk down the street and see people walking about aimlessly, and shops, and cars, and a few dogs, and it all seems to mean nothing and to matter not at all.' Yet Donald Baillie held fast to his faith, which is a very different matter from *feeling* trustful, and many thanked God for his gracious influence.

Many sufferers from recurring depression take some slight but real comfort from the affirmation: 'This also will pass'. There are some medical grounds for this as depression has been called 'a self-terminating illness'. The Christian, even in his darkest hour, can find added comfort in the truth that the darkness that hides God from us does not hide us from God (Psalm 139:12).

> Let me no more my comfort take
> From my frail hold on Thee;
> In this alone rejoice with awe:
> THY MIGHTY GRASP OF ME.

Anxiety—the hidden conflict

CHAPTER 3

Anxiety—the hidden conflict

'I am naturally an anxious person,' a character in an Iris Murdoch novel says to herself, 'stupidly, *wickedly* anxious. Even now as I walk beside this blue sea covered with sugary lights I see it all through a veil of anxiety.'

Many Christians who confess to the same condition also view their anxiety as blameworthy. They are *wickedly* anxious. They feel guilty partly because the New Testament exhorts us not to be anxious but to live in trustful dependence upon our heavenly Father. The word 'anxious' is used in a number of ways, however, and while some worry is sheer self-centredness, what is sometimes called an 'anxiety state' is beyond the immediate control of the will. A person in this condition often has no sizeable problem to fret over; he merely gets worked up over a thousand and one trivialities which even he knows are not the real cause of his trouble. He is the victim of 'floating anxiety' which fastens on to any possible situation which gives him an excuse for worrying. It is worse than useless to tell such a person, as some preachers do, 'If you worry you do not trust, and if you trust you do not worry.' And it is a thousand pities if the sufferer himself adds to his troubles by calling his anxiety *wicked*.

Although the word 'anxiety' can be used in a number of ways, and we may even write to a friend we have not seen for a long time, 'I am very anxious to meet you', in this chapter we shall confine our attention to the anxiety that is provoked not by outward circumstances, but by unconscious conflicts and fears.

In some ways this anxiety resembles the vigilance with which an animal confronts anything new in its environment.

The difference is that whereas in the animal this state of tense alertness lasts for only a few seconds or minutes, in the human being suffering from anxiety it is indefinitely prolonged. Animal vigilance brings the whole organism to a state of preparedness so that if the new object is threatening it may be either attacked or evaded. Fight, flight or submission are the three alternatives from which the animal must choose and vigilance soon gives way to one or other of these courses of action. The anxious human being is usually in a state of vigilance concerning the contents of his own mind and therefore has to live with this continually. Vigilance becomes chronic.

It is also clear that animals endeavour to avoid the painful experience of extreme fright by developing a capacity to perceive signals of impending danger long before the danger actually materialises. They do not need to see their enemy before they prepare for emergency action: they merely need the slightest smell of him carried on the wind. This notion of 'signal-anxiety' has also been applied to human beings who learn to guard against memories, emotions and desires which they fear. So it is possible to be in a highly anxious state without having a clue as to what it is we dread. It is the combination of vigilance and inaction which makes the anxiety state so painful.

It is in an attempt to end this intolerable suspense that sometimes the person suffering from an anxiety state unconsciously projects his anxiety on to some exterior object or situation. When we simply cannot admit to consciousness what we really fear, we may translate our anxiety into a dread of open spaces, or heights, or knives, or cats, or indeed, almost any object under the sun. These fears are called phobias and are very common. The sufferer recognises how irrational his phobia is and is humiliated by his inability to conquer it. Yet despite the fact that a phobia may severely restrict a person's life it also serves the useful purpose of limiting the area of anxiety. The person suffering from claustrophobia will be driven to sheer panic by the prospect of travelling in a lift or a crowded train, but away from these situations he is comparatively free from acute anxiety.

Anxiety which has its origin deep in the unconscious may also become focused upon our bodies so that we become hypochondriacs, always imagining we have some serious and probably fatal illness. Even after exhaustive medical tests and repeated assurances some sufferers remain convinced that they are physically ill. Despite the very real distress this causes them, it is preferable to confronting the faceless enemy of undefined anxiety, the panic about which we can do nothing for we are ignorant of its cause.

It is very easy for the anxious person to become obsessed with his physical health, not only because this serves to distract his attention from the real cause of his anxiety, but because he usually does have a number of physical symptoms to contend with. Palpitations, headaches, dizziness, digestive upsets, breathlessness, an unassuagable thirst, sundry pains caused by muscular tension: all these are common accompaniments to an anxiety state. Needless to say, these symptoms can also indicate physical illnesses such as diabetes or disorders of the thyroid gland. We should never be our own diagnostician in these matters.

The agitated, tense person who has phobias or presents these physical symptoms is disturbed because deep-seated conflict is erupting into consciousness, even though in a disguised form. He knows full well that all is not well in his inner life. Some persons who basically have the same deep conflicts, however, have no symptoms except persistent fatigue. This is because unconsciously they are expending all their energy in totally repressing the conflict which is only partially repressed in the obviously anxious person.

How can we cope with anxiety? The answer to this question will depend largely, as we suggested in the case of depression, on the severity of the condition. Once anxiety has reached a certain pitch of intensity we shall be wise to seek the help of our doctor and, in some instances, psychotherapy which aims to uncover the unconscious conflicts may be necessary.

There are, however, some things we can do to help ourselves in a mild anxiety state and which would also enable us to co-operate effectively with our doctor if we need medical or psychiatric treatment. Anxiety can be lessened by physical and psychological means and in addition to this two-pronged approach the Christian will seek to draw on spiritual resources.

*   *   *

The most common physical treatment for an anxiety state is the vast range of tranquillisers which the general practioner is now able to prescribe. Some people object to using these drugs because they imagine they will be reduced to a drowsy, half-conscious state in which their work will be impaired. Most of these tranquillisers, however, can be taken without noticeably lessening concentration and alertness.

Another objection sometimes raised against the use of tranquillisers is that they dampen down the internal conflict so that the chances of coming to terms with the real cause of anxiety is reduced. There is some truth in this, but it has to be recognised that not everyone can or should undergo extensive psychotherapy. Apart from the fact that there are simply not enough psychotherapists to deal with even the severe mental and emotional illnesses, it might take years to get to the root of some anxieties.

Many anxiety states are temporary conditions brought on when shock, overwork or physical illness have weakened our resistance against long-buried fears and conflicts. The best treatment for by far the greater number of anxiety states is one which strengthens these barriers and enables us to continue life as before. As we shall see in a later chapter on 'self-awareness', nobody can know all the truth about himself. Sometimes we must be content to allow a neurotic symptom to be treated without discovering what it is all about. We must, of course, allow our doctor to be the best judge of what treatment we need.

Anxiety can sometimes be considerably reduced by regular relaxation, and many sufferers have achieved quite startling results in this way. This is because, although anxiety originates in the mind, it doesn't stay there. It produces that state of physical tenseness which ideally prepares the animal for a fight or flight, but since neither course is open to the human being the result is merely mounting panic.

To understand how relaxation helps to diminish anxiety we need to recognise how closely mind and body react upon each other when we are emotionally disturbed. In his book, *Relaxation, A Key to Better Living*, J. Macdonald Wallace describes the physical 'alarm reaction' which accompanies the emotions of fear, anger or anxiety, beginning in the hypothalamus, a part of the brain. 'The alarm is triggered off in the hypothalamus, and a whole host of things happen. From the motor area, signals are sent to muscles to tense, ready to fight or to flee—as many muscles, and as much tension, as the situation seems to require. Instantly, from the hypothalamus, urgent signals are sent by the sympathetic nervous system to all other systems to bolster up the muscles in their readiness. The heart beats faster and more strongly; breathing becomes quicker and more shallow; tiny blood vessels contract to shut off the blood supply from the digestive system and direct it to the active muscles; the muscular walls of the gullet, the stomach and the intestines may go into spasm, producing the nauseating feeling of "butterflies"; blood pressure is raised; the sweat glands open up, and the salivary glands dry up; more red blood cells are pumped into the circulating blood from the spleen in order to supply more oxygen to the muscles, and more sugar is released from the liver to supply the necessary energy to the muscles. Vomiting or urination may occur. At the same time, an instant signal is sent to the adrenal gland to release more adrenalin into the blood stream. The adrenalin continues to maintain all the above reactions which were initiated by the sympathetic nervous system.'

Nearly all these reactions are completely beyond our conscious control, *except the reaction of muscular tension*. We cannot stop our adrenal gland from secreting adrenalin but we can deliberately untense our muscles. Moreover, relaxing our muscles cuts down the electrical excitement in the nervous system and inhibits the 'alarm reaction' of the sympathetic nervous system described above, including the activity of the adrenal gland.

Unfortunately muscular tension can become so chronic that we are unaware of just how tense our muscles are. Part of the technique of relaxation consists in learning to recognise varying degrees of tension throughout the body. Chronic muscular tension, which began because alarm signals were received from the mind, has the effect of sending back alarm signals. The result is an escalation of panic and anxiety.

The regular and conscientious practice of relaxation can break into this vicious circle with dramatic effects. However, this sounds much easier than it is and most people need the help of a simple but well-written book describing the technique. These can be bought for a few shillings or borrowed from the library.

* * *

Anxiety can be greatly reduced by tranquillisers, and some people attain an even greater degree of equilibrium by the regular practice of relaxation. Yet the basic cause of anxiety is psychological. Can we do anything to help ourselves at this level?

We have already indicated that whereas the tense, alert animal is scrutinising his environment for danger, the human being with an anxiety state is guarding against something in

44

his own mind. This is usually a deeply buried conflict which was split off from consciousness in early life and cannot be recovered by any effort of will. The two aspects of personality which are most likely to undergo this splitting off, or repression as it is usually called, are sexuality and aggression.

If we could bring to consciousness our repressed conflicts we should no longer suffer from an anxiety state. We might well have other worries on our hands, such as coming to terms with intense hostility we did not know we possessed, or assimilating into our personalities desires we had previously denied. These concerns would give us cause for careful and perhaps agonising thought, but they would not make us tensely vigilant or give rise to neurotic symptoms.

It follows that the more we get to understand ourselves the less anxious we shall be. However, this is not as simple as it sounds. Self-knowledge is the attainment of a lifetime and the anxious person always has particularly stubborn resistances to overcome in becoming more aware of what goes on in the depths of his personality.

We can, however, begin the journey even though it will be a long time before we arrive. It is important to recognise that we do not attain self-awareness by protracted sessions of introspection, nor by trying to force the pace. Great patience is called for, as well as the humble recognition that self-deception is always a possibility.

More will be said about attaining self-awareness in a later chapter. Here we will say no more than that a person will learn more of the truth about himself by a gentle and kindly watchfulness over his spontaneous reactions, than by constant self-absorption. Especially will this be so if he acquaints himself with some elementary knowledge of the way human personality works.

If, for instance, we grasp the principle that our keenest antagonisms are directed against that in other people which reminds us of the unacknowledged parts of ourselves we shall be in a position to learn a great deal from our hostile feelings towards others. Similarly, when we know that nearly all compulsively exaggerated behaviour is an inner defence erected by the personality to guard against the opposite tendency, we shall know that our excessive compliance masks an aggression we dare not feel, our over-assertiveness a timidity we thought we had long since overcome, and our prudery defends us against what C. S. Lewis once called 'a bedlam of lusts'.

Learning the truth about oneself calls for patient watchfulness. It also requires humility, the humility which recognises that we share with the whole human family certain basic drives which in themselves are morally neutral. It is what we do with these drives that makes us moral or immoral. But in origin our instincts are concerned only with *our* safety and *our* pleasure.

What prevents some religious people from learning to know themselves is an unrealistic notion of their own nature. They despise the self-assertion and sensuality which are a part of a full personality and which, in a mature person, contribute richly to his usefulness.

Neurosis is an inner cleavage', claimed Carl Jung, 'the state of being at war with oneself.' When a country is rent by civil war, claimed this pioneer psychotherapist, 'this state is to be cured by the Christian virtue of forgiveness for those who hate us. That which we try with the conviction of good Christians to apply to external situations, we must apply to the inner state in the treatment of neurosis.' Modern man wants to learn 'how he is to reconcile himself to his own nature—how he is to love the enemy in his own heart and call the wolf his brother.'

The refusal to face ourselves at depth results in the unacknowledged aspects of our personality taking on a more fearsome and persistent role. James Hillman writes, 'In the startling dreams of terror, of ugly images and cruelties, we often forget that the unconscious shows the face which we show it. It is like a mirror. If I flee, it pursues. If I am high up, it is an abyss below. If I am too noble, it sends me nasty dreams. And if I turn my back, it attracts and tempts me to turn and look with seductive images. The gulf between consciousness and the unconscious narrows as we are able to feel for it and give to it, as we are able to live with it as a friend.'

It has long been recognised that we can more easily come to terms with ourselves in a relationship with someone who is able to accept us fully. The undoubted success of spiritual direction in some branches of the Christian church owes much to this fact, and upon it is built most forms of psychotherapy. We often imagine that when we have admitted the truth to ourselves we are well on the road to self-knowledge. Yet until we have shared this truth with another person it remains an insight all too easily lost.

It follows that if we are plagued with anxiety we should seek a wise and competent counsellor with whom we can share our problem. It is also true that every good and satisfying relationship in which we can be fully honest assists the healing process in which rejected aspects of our personality are integrated into the whole self.

*   *   *

Having considered what can be done on both the physical and mental levels to diminish anxiety, it remains to ask: Has religious faith a specific contribution to make? We shall consider its relationship to the whole range of emotional problems at the end of this book. Here it is sufficient to suggest its particular relevance to anxiety.

The kind of anxiety we have been considering has its origins in depths of the mind beyond our immediate access. An anxiety state is provoked, not by physical danger in the environment, but by conflicts and emotions which threaten to disrupt our mental equilibrium. Before these can be admitted to consciousness we often need to change our ideas about ourselves. Emotions which we would have said are just 'not us' have to be admitted as playing a very important role in our personalities, even if from below the level of consciousness.

This can be an agonising process. Frequently it is possible only in the company of a wise and sympathetic counsellor. Yet the Christian can surely be helped in this direction if he understands his religion aright. The God revealed to us in Jesus is not a God who is easily shocked. In the Gospel narratives we see Him facing the very worst in human nature with undiminished love and compassion. Surely, in His presence we can come to terms with the most unlovely aspects of ourselves and know that we are still accepted, not because of what we are, but because of who God is.

It is only when our religion is tainted with moralism that it offers us no help in facing anxiety. When our acceptance with God is thought to depend upon being at least fairly respectable persons, we simply dare not admit the buried rage, hatred and lust into consciousness. The result is that these emotions get projected on to other people, so distorting our whole outlook, and we remain tense, anxious people, divided against ourselves, ever vigilant lest the truth should emerge in an unguarded moment.

In his book *Prescription for Anxiety* Leslie Weatherhead has two chapters which show how the truth about ourselves and the truth about God both serve to lessen anxiety. The God revealed in Christ is One who can help us to face our anxiety just because in His presence we can be fully ourselves without fear of losing His love. Unfortunately, we all tend to expect from God the harsh disapproval of our negative feelings that we early experienced from people. We *know* that God is loving and accepting; we *feel* that He is rejecting and severe. We must recognise that these feelings reflect, not God's attitude to us, but our own past experience with people who had too much anxiety of their own to be able to face calmly our childish tantrums.

It is one of the most important functions of prayer and worship to help us assimilate into the very depths of our being the truth about God manifested to us in Jesus Christ. This, as we shall see in a later chapter, frees our relationship with God from childish fantasies and supports us in our quest for self-understanding.

Deviant sex —
     the maimed instinct

CHAPTER 4

Deviant sex—
the maimed instinct

Anyone with experience of personal counselling knows the deep humiliation suffered by those with sexual problems. Usually, it is only after years of fruitless struggle and unhappiness that a person will share with someone else his battle with deviant desires or obsessive fantasies. The reason for this reluctance is easy to understand. For one thing, a sex problem is often an indication of what is wrong with the whole personality. Therefore, to reveal to another person the nature of our sexual drives is to expose ourselves at great depth.

This, however, is not the only reason why many prefer to struggle on in lonely isolation. Despite the freedom with which these matters are discussed and the far more enlightened view now prevailing towards sexual problems, it is still true that many religious people attach far greater guilt to failure in this than in any other realm. A man will confess his bad temper, which casts gloom and fear over his whole family, with comparative ease. His sexual obsession which may well make nobody unhappy but himself, he will admit only with great shame and confusion.

There is no doubt whatsoever that these problems intensify in isolation, and are somewhat diminished when we share them with another person. It is therefore regrettable that some Christians have a reputation for being far too easily shocked in these matters: consequently more sufferers are now turning to doctors, psychiatrists, marriage guidance counsellors, Samaritans and similar helping agencies.

It is not only 'religious' attitudes, however, which tend to load people who have sexual difficulties with unproductive guilt. Secular society must bear a large proportion of the blame. For the widespread notion—fostered in films, plays and novels—that sexual fulfilment is the one supreme bliss evokes deep inferiority in those to whom this is denied. Much contemporary literature, and even some sex manuals, creates a totally false concept of what is the norm in terms of sexual activity. Those who do not measure up to this, either in the frequency of their sexual activity or the satisfaction they gain from it, are made unnecessarily anxious in a way that would never have occurred when sex was rarely discussed. Personnel selection officers, for instance, claim that unmarried people are often over-eager to assure them that they have a lively sex life in order to avoid the inference that, by current standards, they are somewhat deficient.

Although in this chapter we shall briefly consider the difficulties of the adolescent who has to deal with normal sexual frustration because he is physically mature many years before he can get married, we are more concerned with the person for whom sex is a *permanent* 'problem'. Either this manifests itself in some form of deviation, so that his sexual drives are directed to an inappropriate goal (e.g. a member of his own sex as in homosexuality, the infliction or the suffering of pain as in sado-masochism, the observation of sexual activity in others as in voyeurism) or else his sexuality is so fraught with anxiety that it becomes obsessive. We have all had the experience in which a particular tune, often one we do not particularly like, keeps running through our mind. We seem powerless to dismiss this repetitive dirge, and when we are at last free it is never by an act of will on our part. The person with a sexual obsession is in a like state.

The person with a sexual problem is far more often deprived than depraved. He is frequently very lonely and dogged by inferiority. If, as a great deal of evidence suggests, the origins of most of these problems lie far back in childhood, it is clear that a Christian may suffer deviant impulses as well as anyone else. Nor is anyone automatically

54

relieved of his difficulty by becoming a Christian. A homosexual does not become heterosexual in his *desires* by committing his life to Christ.

First, we will briefly look at some of the causes of sexual deviation and obsession. Perhaps more than with any other emotional problem, the sufferer can find tremendous relief, and even be set on the way to a solution, by seeing the whole situation in terms of cause and effect rather than in terms of temptation and sin.

As already indicated, there is such a thing as normal, healthy sexual frustration which may range from a slight restlessness to a deeply disturbing craving. As naturally as a thirsty man finds himself constantly imagining streams of water so a sexually deprived man may find erotic fantasies persistently encroaching upon his thoughts. This is more true for men than for most women, in that they are quickly aroused by visual stimuli, but some women also have great difficulty in handling clamorously urgent desires.

Difficult though this frustration may be to handle, it is due to the normal functioning of the sexual appetite, not its malfunctioning as in the sexual deviations. It is particularly the problem of the growing young man. The important thing to recognise is the essentially temporary nature of these difficulties. Perhaps the greatest danger of this period is that the purely physical side of the sexual relationship, just because this is where the tension is felt, will become detached from its wider context of loving tenderness and mutuality. One psychiatrist used to advise young men, 'Don't turn away in disgust from your fantasies. Carry them through to their obvious conclusion. See the girl bearing and nursing your child. In this way keep sex in its proper context. Recognise that it is not an end in itself but part of a permanent loving relationship.'

A chapter on 'Deviant Sex' is not the place to deal at length with masturbation, yet as this still arouses considerable unhappiness among many people it cannot be entirely overlooked. Perhaps the best way to view the practice is to see it as a regression, a return to the self-comforting of childhood, which we fall into most easily when growing-up becomes difficult and problematic. It is certain that to increase the sense of guilt which attaches to the practice is *always* to increase the compulsiveness of the desire, and that to encourage every outgoing interest, and particularly every healthy relationship, is a more effective way of dealing with it than to summon up every ounce of will power.

When we turn from the temporary difficulties of the maturing adolescent to the deviant or the sex-obsessed we are dealing with far more intractable problems because they involve the whole personality. For the deviant, the way to a loving relationship with a member of the opposite sex is blocked by guilt and fear. Consequently, his sexual impulse fastens on some substitute which does not provoke anxiety. For the sex-obsessed, the way is not entirely blocked but is fraught with such uncertainty and unconscious doubt that the whole subject becomes a constant preoccupation as the mind tries, without much success, to unravel its tangled threads.

Many psychotherapists would agree with Anthony Storr that the deviations have their origin in sexual guilt and sexual inferiority instilled at a very early age. John Wain, in his autobiography *Sprightly Running*, points to one way in which sex can become riddled with unhappy, guilt-provoking associations: 'In the limited vocabulary of children (and I don't think it has changed since 1930, the year I am speaking of) there are two very potent words: "rude" and "rough". "Rude" means not only impolite, but obscene; an equation easy to make in the nursery, because impolite behaviour, in that setting, *is* usually obscene, usually concerned with the faeces or the private organs in some way. Children haven't the wit to be insulting in a polite way, nor, since their adult sex functions have not begun, have they the means of being obscene in any way but an insulting or threatening way. So "rude" means things like spitting out your food on the tablecloth, and also walking about the room with no trousers on. I suppose child psychologists, in elaborate tomes I have not read, are on to this problem, but I should like to remark as a layman that this coupling of differing activities under the one heading must have very far-reaching effects. A lot of things a child is taught to call "rude" are in fact simply manifestations of nascent sexuality; this must be, at any rate partly, the reason why so many people carry through life the conviction that sexual activity is the exact equivalent of spitting your food on the tablecloth (cf. the expression "clean-living", meaning "celibate", with its strong implication that non-celibates are living dirtily.).'

Even when a child is not made to feel guilty about sex by shocked parental reaction to his natural explorations of his own body, and the bodies of his friends, he can come to suspect that there is something inherently 'bad' about the subject by the mere absence of any positive attitudes to sexuality. Silence may be as effective as prohibition in creating negative associations.

Sexual guilt may be absorbed from the environment. Sexual inferiority is frequently due to a childhood failure to identify fully with a parent of the same sex who is confidently happy in his or her role. If father is remote and unfriendly, or even absent: if mother is always at odds with her lot as a woman, or in fact plays the dominant role in her marriage, then a child has utmost difficulty in progressing towards assured masculinity or femininity. As Simone de Beauvoir writes, 'One is not born a woman, one becomes a woman.' The same is true for the man and the reason why people of both sexes fail to achieve confident masculinity and femininity is due to this early breakdown in identification.

That multitudes of people are unsure of their sexual identity is maintained by Vance Packard in *The Hidden*

Persuaders when he writes, 'The motivational analysts began finding that a major sexual need of both men and women in America at the mid-century was sexual reassurance. Women by the millions were yearning for evidence that they were still basically feminine and men by the millions were yearning for evidence that they were still indisputably and virulently masculine.'

Many of us suffer to some extent from sexual guilt and sexual inferiority, but when these reach certain proportions the way to a full relationship with the opposite sex is blocked. It is then a person is unconsciously driven to find substitutes in the outer world or in the inner world of fantasy.

One particularly unhappy result of sexual guilt is that it makes it impossible for the person to integrate his feelings of loving affection with his sexual desires. This happens more frequently in men though it is by no means rare in women. Freudian psychology explains this fact by reference to the problems the growing boy has of coping with the sexual feelings he has towards his mother. Whether or not we accept the Freudian explanation, it can happen that a man is sexually aroused by women he otherwise despises, and impotent with a woman he truly loves.

One form this separation of love from sex takes is the pornography which regards woman as a mere plaything, a sexual object. The men to whom this appeals find it impossible to relate mentally and physically to one woman. They want a woman who serves no other function than that of satisfying male desire. Another reason why pornography, and anything which stimulates lively sexual fantasy, has such a strong appeal to some men is that in the realm of imagination a man's actual potency is not challenged. He can retain his illusions about being 'a great lover' without having these destroyed by a real encounter with a real woman. Here again we see the outcroppings of anxious inferiority.

Sexual guilt has the further result of making us dishonest

about our desires. The sincerely religious person, anxious to keep a clear conscience, tends to impose on himself an absolute prohibition against sexual feelings. Now it is a psychological law that 'demands build up when needs are not admitted.' The person who can admit his desires to consciousness always has the option of saying no to them. The person who cannot admit his desires, because even the desire makes him feel guilty, finds he is suddenly confronted by uncontrollable demands.

These, then, are some of the ways in which a person may become the victim of deviant desires or be plagued by unwanted fantasies. Unfortunately, although knowing how these problems originate may lessen our guilt, it may leave our compulsions unchanged. How should this situation be faced?

* * *

We should begin by recognising that the lessening of guilt is itself therapeutic. Moralists are always afraid that when guilt is diminished a person will totally capitulate to his compulsions. In fact, the reverse is true. The more guilty a person feels the less resistance he is able to offer. This is the failure of moralism which the apostle Paul so clearly exposed in his letter to the church at Rome. The moral struggle is self-defeating when it is merely an attempt to avoid condemnation.

For the Christian, the kind of guilt we are considering here is dealt with in two ways. Firstly, by the honest recognition that a person is usually no more responsible for deviant sexual desires than he is responsible for being born with a physical impediment. God does not want us to take responsibility for things we cannot help. Irrational guilt cannot be forgiven for there is nothing to forgive. It can only be resolutely disclaimed. Secondly, in so far as we have all failed to love God with our whole being and our neighbours as ourselves we must seek and accept the forgiveness of God. Then there should be no more self-accusings. Remember that a guilt-burdened mind is more prey to unhealthy obsessions than one which rejoices in the pardon and loving acceptance of God.

We must also recognise the severe limitations of mere will-power in these matters. Otherwise we shall go on indefinitely believing that if only we tried a little harder, exercised a more rigorous watch upon our minds, we would rid ourselves of every undesirable thought and impulse. Yet screwing up the last ounce of will-power is the least successful way of approaching these difficulties, and the longer we retain the illusion that more effort is what we need the longer we postpone taking more effective measures.

In Boris Pasternak's *Doctor Zhivago* a character says, 'I think that if the beast who sleeps in man could be held down by threats—any kind of threat, whether of jail or of retribution after death—then the highest emblem of humanity would be the lion tamer in the circus with his whip, not the self-sacrificing preacher.'

We help ourselves most not by making a direct attack upon what we may call our 'problem', but by recognising that the more *attention* we give to this, even in prayer, the more persistent and obsessive it will become. We do more by sharing our difficulties with a wise friend, by strengthening our relationships with other people, and by developing every healthy interest to the full, than we ever do by making resolves or by anxious preparation for the next onslaught of 'temptation'.

We need to see this particular difficulty in the much larger perspective of our Christian discipleship. In their book *Stones or Bread* Gerald Vann and P.K. Meagher say, 'Because fallen human nature is what it is, we must expect, unless we are very fortunate and unusual people, to be tempted in one way or another on the sense level, and to be tempted often, perhaps continuously, perhaps obsessively. And if that is the case we must expect also, unless we are very sure of ourselves, that sometimes we shall fail. Now if these difficulties are seen in their proper perspective as one element in the totality of the Christian life, they can be dealt with sanely and constructively. When we fall, in this as in any other context, the only reasonable thing is to pick ourselves up again—or rather, to beg God to pick us up again—and to make a fresh start, using our failure as a means to humility and a greater reliance upon God, but not at all as an invitation to discouragement or gnawing anxiety.'

Unfortunately, people with sexual difficulties all too often see the Christian life only in terms of their particular problem. Chastity is to them the one important virtue. Failure here is total failure: success here is total success. Yet if we consider the way Jesus attacked the Scribes and the Pharisees, and offered His friendship to moral outcasts, this alone would adjust this all-too-narrow view of the good life. Few things are more important to people oppressed by sexual temptations than to switch their attention from the battle with their fantasies and compulsions to the far larger issues of loving one's neighbour and becoming, at *every* level, more like Christ.

Since sexual deviations are sometimes the most intractable of personality problems, and even the prolonged therapy available to only a small minority of patients does not always result in a complete 'cure', the Christian so afflicted must find in the loving acceptance of God a basis for self-acceptance. This does not mean a moral compromise but a recognition that, no matter how completely dedicated to God is the conscious will, unconscious conflicts still persist in the form of unwelcome obsessions and desires. Karl Rahner, the Roman Catholic theologian, suggests that although we should not minimise our personal defects, there are times when these 'must just be accepted and suffered through, since there is such a thing as a truly Christian suffering at the hands of one's defects.'

A much earlier spiritual guide, John Nicholas Grou, similarly advised the kind of patient, gentle persistence which is especially appropriate for anyone who has to contend with deep-rooted compulsions. Writing of the truly devout man he said, 'He has made a determination, once for all, to refuse nothing to God, to grant nothing to self-love, and never to commit a voluntary fault; but he does not perplex himself; he goes on courageously; he is not too particular. If he falls into a fault, he does not get distressed; he humbles himself at the sight of his own weakness; he gets up again, and thinks no more about it. He is not astonished at his weaknesses, at his falls, at his imperfections; he is never discouraged. He knows that he can do nothing but that God can do everything. He does not rely upon his own good thoughts and resolutions, but simply upon the grace and goodness of God. If he were to fall a hundred times a day, he would not despair; but he would stretch out his hands lovingly to God, and beg of Him to lift him up and take pity on him.'

If at the root of most sexual problems there is a tragic divorce between love and sex then our most pressing need is not to wage war upon our physical desires but to become more deeply and genuinely loving in all our relationships. We cannot do this to order, and we shall look at the difficulties in a later chapter. The Christian finds that, with the help that comes from communion with God, he can steadily move in this direction.

Jealousy—the deprived infant

CHAPTER 5

Jealousy—the deprived infant

An old story tells of a hermit whose sanctity made him impervious to the assaults of all the demons assigned to tempt him. Finally, the devil himself decided to take a hand and whispered that the hermit's brother had just been made Bishop of Alexandria. Sadly, the saint who had withstood all other temptations, fell into the sin of jealousy.

It is typical of the complexities of human nature, that often the person with least grounds for envy is the one who suffers the agony of this 'rebel emotion'. Frequently it is the gifted man who is jealous of the colleague who is only marginally more competent: the beautiful woman who envies the one woman in a large company who outshines her.

Unhappily, jealousy sometimes poisons the spirits of those engaged in the most worth-while service. At great personal cost a man may pioneer work in some area of human need, working for years on his own. Others imagine his one desire is for fellow-workers to ease the burden and bring the stimulus of new ideas. Yet when these colleagues at long last appear they are treated as trespassers and their success only grudgingly admitted.

Jealousy is unmitigated misery. Some emotions—like hatred, pride or lust—carry with them at least some tinge of pleasure or release. The envious person is, however, always in the toils of anguish. To feel jealous is invariably humiliating and this fact may give a clue to the deep roots of this emotion, as we shall see later.

In Dante's purgatory the envious sit like blind beggars by a wall, their eyelids sewed shut. Jealousy shuts us in on ourselves, not only because it is essentially a self-obsessed emotion, but because it is one we find it impossible to communicate or confess. He was either a cynic or a courageous man who admitted, 'I find no difficulty in sympathising with my friends in their misfortune; what is difficult is sympathising with them in their good fortune.'

Few can be as honest as this about their jealousies, or even rise to the self-revelation of the prayer by Thomas Fuller: 'Lord, I perceive my soul deeply guilty of envy . . . I had rather Thy work were undone than done better by another than by myself! . . . Dispossess me, Lord, of this bad spirit, and turn my envy into holy emulation; . . . yea, make other men's gifts to be mine, by making me thankful to Thee for them.'

As with the other 'rebel emotions' we are considering jealousy may exist in those comparatively mild forms with which we are all at some time acquainted, or become so obsessive and disabling as to constitute a severe psychological disturbance. This is not to say that if we harbour our envy we shall eventually have a mental breakdown, for there is a qualitative difference between the envy that most of us feel and the delusional jealousy which calls for skilled treatment.

At the more superficial level our envy is obviously related to our expectation. A society which encourages its members in the conviction that considerable material possessions—a semi-detached house, a car, a fridge, a substantial bank balance—are theirs by right stimulates envy in the minds of those who lack these possessions. One of the greatest advances of this century has been the recognition that equality of opportunity is every man's right. Yet as an unexpected by-product of this new sense of social justice we may be making it more difficult for people to handle their jealousy. 'Our fever for equality is one of the most serious ills of our age . . . In the end, nobody finds himself able to stand being unequal to anyone else in anything.' We may question the first part of this statement of Gustave Thibon, while recognising the truth in the second part.

Undoubtedly, life in the affluent countries is a breeding ground for jealousy. Some forms of advertising even harness this emotion as the motivation for buying the goods they wish to sell.

Another cause of jealousy is our tendency to idealise other people's lives and assume that whereas we are often plagued with self-doubt, they walk with supreme confidence through the world, that while we have to wrestle with all kinds of unlovely emotions, they always feel serene and loving.

In David Scott Blackhall's delightful book, *This House had Windows*, the author recalls an incident concerning a blind man which considerably helped him when later he lost his own sight. On a periodic visit to his home town, he was talking over old times with a group of friends when they were joined by a recently-blinded young man. The young man mistook David Blackhall for his brother, then became terribly confused about his mistake, and finally added, 'I didn't expect to find David here. I know he's got something I haven't got.' Instead of the embarrassed silence which one might have expected to follow this remark, an older man immediately said, 'You don't know who is better off than you are and you don't know who is worse off. Now shut up!'

'Perhaps you will think that this was an unkind thing to say', comments David Blackhall. 'I remember thinking at the time that it was exactly the right thing to say and it needed a lot of courage to say it.' Then, referring to the time when he lost his own sight, he adds, 'When I came out of hospital, I said to myself, "You don't know who is better off than you are and you don't know who is worse off. Now shut up!" I brushed my hair and I straightened my tie and I went back to the office.'

We may think that such masterly conquest of self-pity would be beyond us, yet it is worth noting that it was linked with this very valuable insight, which those who know anything of the inner lives of other people would confirm a thousand times over, 'You don't know who is better off than you and you don't know who is worse off.' How ironic that if we knew the whole truth about the lives of many of those we envy we would not change places with them for anything!

Jealousy is often caused by the false expectations which a consumer society deliberately engenders in us, or by the tendency to idealise the experience of other people. Yet when we have done our very best to rid our hearts of the lie that possessions, promotion and status are essential to our happiness, and when we have achieved a more realistic view of life, recognising that nobody finds life easy or escapes deep hurt, we may still be plagued by this humiliating jealousy.

What more can we do? First, it is crucial that we face our jealousy and acknowledge it, *and this may well mean acknowledging it to someone else*. If we fail to do this our jealousy could easily go underground but, like all repressed emotions, it will not thereby cease to influence us. Instead of feeling jealous of the successful colleague we shall begin to find 'reasons' for distrusting him. Instead of envying his competence we shall call in question his character. 'He is an excellent business man,' we say, 'but he must be hell to live with!' 'She is giving wonderful service,' we grudgingly admit, 'but you know *why*, don't you?'

Even though we may not drive our envy underground, if we still insist on struggling with it alone, there is the further danger that it will become disproportionate, as emotions suffered in solitude generally do. Evelyn Ayrault was born a cripple, and was naturally envious of her healthy sister. However, she loved her sister dearly and the infrequent pangs of jealousy did not spoil their relationship. Her parents, however, spoke so much of the danger of jealousy that they made the situation worse. Evelyn Ayrault writes, 'Hearing from them how bad it was for me to envy my sister made a deep impression on my mind. Soon I began to fear my own envy and magnify it too.'

Confessing one's envy may be a humbling experience, but

it will help us to get it in proportion, and if we are fortunate enough to have a wise counsellor in whom to confide he may assist us to trace our bitterness to its roots and to relate it to other parts of our personality. Sometimes we have to admit our faults to another before there is any deeply-felt validity in admitting them to ourselves. Nevertheless this honesty requires courage.

Writing in his journal, Dag Hammarskjöld confessed, 'In spite of everything, your bitterness because others are enjoying what you are denied is always ready to flare up. At best it may lie dormant for a couple of sunny days. Yet, even at this unspeakably shabby level, it is still an expression of the real bitterness of death—the fact that others are allowed to go on living.'

Ideally, it is good to do more than face our jealousy or even to record it, like Dag Hammarskjöld, in a personal journal. If we can share it with some helpful friend it could be decisive in enabling us to dispel, or at least modify, our feelings. Tracking a persistent tendency to jealousy to its root cause will be more difficult, sometimes impossible.

We have said that the realisation that jealousy is a humiliating emotion gives us a clue to its origin. It is associated with weakness, the weakness of the child. It was then that we were totally dependent upon others, not only for warmth, food and physical security, but also for love. If they (as we then thought) chose to withdraw their affection we were utterly powerless to do anything about it. In the very nature of things every child at some time has felt left alone, forsaken and bereft. If, added to this feeling, there is the conviction that the supplies of well-being are now directed elsewhere, so that others are receiving the bounty which we are denied, then here is the seed bed of a jealous temperament in later life.

It is hard for us as adults, for instance, to imagine ourselves into the situation of a child when the first baby brother or sister arrives. If, sometimes unavoidably, this requires a withdrawal of mother's presence and apparently of her affection, something he has never had to share with another child in the whole of his life before, this will seem nothing less than a major catastrophe.

It is important to see that the basic grievance which underlies all other grievances is that we feel we are not loved, or not sufficiently loved. Status, possessions, promotion and all the other things which provoke us to jealousy are essentially substitutes for affection. If this seems an unlikely account of the jealous temperament, because many jealous people are surrounded by affection, then we must remember that if ever, in early life, the spirit has faced the ultimate desolation of feeling unloved (however unjustified this was), then that memory continues to reverberate in the unconscious mind throughout the rest of life. It lies dormant until that time when we are faced with loss and we feel our security threatened. This deep, unacknowledged fear that we are not loved for ourselves is why some people's desire for reassurance is utterly insatiable. They *never* can receive sufficient reassurance, for the secret anguish is far too fearful to be faced, and therefore it is little modified by present experience. The pain usually remains in the deep unconscious mind, sending up its anxious signals whenever life threatens to repeat its dreadful deception.

Jealousy is closely linked with a sense of inferiority. The person who lacks confidence in himself naturally fears rivals. He doubts his ability to retain the affection of his wife, or his friends, when there are obviously so many more attractive people around. He is sure that he must be displaced in his work when others are clearly more competent.

Because jealousy so often arises from inferiority it is self-defeating to feel guilty about this emotion. This merely increases inferiority (for guilt and inferiority are twins) and aggravates the very condition which requires alleviation. So, in trying to trace the roots of envy, it is better to try to understand our sense of inferiority than to tackle our jealousy.

Like all morbid emotions, envy and jealousy become intensified in isolation and are diminished by every good healthy relationship we maintain or develop. This is why, tragically, people can first feel the full impact of jealousy when, later in life, they lose those who have been dear to them through the years.

Jealousy can rage most furiously in the marriage relationship and it is here that some would suggest it may be perfectly justified. A husband or wife may be jealous, not only of a sexual rival, but even of the partner's interests, achievements, work and friends. This is most likely where marriage has been entered into in order to gain some sense of identity through the partner, where what is sought is not a relationship between two people but a unity which destroys individuality. One psychotherapist said that the best prescription for a happy marriage is not, 'We two are one', but 'We two are three'—each one his individual self and also the relationship created between us.

Where identity and not relationship is being sought a man or woman will naturally feel threatened by an interest, task or pleasure which belongs exclusively to the other partner. The misery caused by this sort of envy, with all its potential destructiveness, is immense and it is a frequent cause of marriage breakdown. Even here, the answer is not to be found in increasing the jealous person's sense of guilt, but in skilled counselling and therapy. The victim of such destructive emotions will frequently complain that there is absolutely nothing he can do to modify his feelings. To a large extent this is true. Perhaps the one thing he can sometimes undertake, and this will require courage of a high order, is to admit his need of outside help and face in the presence of another his deep humiliation.

Jealousy of a potential or actual rival for our partner's affection may be thought the one instance where the emotion serves as a useful danger signal. Though even here, one would need eventually to work through to a more creative way of dealing with the problem. Feeling jealous does not heal a relationship, and where there has actually been some loss of affection one has to enquire into the quality of the marriage and seek for constructive ways of improving it, ultimately the only way of securing it against breakdown.

Groundless jealousy, a frequently-found and very persistent trait, may have several causes. A man or woman who feels, even without cause, some insecurity in their masculine or feminine role will obviously be more fearful of rivals. When jealousy is linked with suspicious delusions, however, it is nearly always a sign that the jealous person has displaced his or her own sexuality, or desire for freedom, on to the partner. Because he (or she) cannot recognise the waywardness of his own desires, he becomes convinced that his partner is acting out what he himself has repressed. Here again, some outside help is obviously called for.

People vary in their ability to find healing for this distress in their religious faith. It would be comforting to say that if only the sufferer will at this point believe in the love of God, then all sense of deprivation and inferiority will disappear: comforting but untrue. Perhaps a great deal depends upon how deeply a person feels, rather than intellectually asserts, the reality of a personal God. But one thing is sure, there are some believers who say in effect: 'Do not talk to me about the love of God. I want to be loved by my fellows, and if I feel uncared for at this level the love of God is no compensation.' Others, on the other hand, find deep comfort in the assurance of God's infinite and unconditioned love.

Perhaps this very fact, that many find the assurance of God's love in itself inadequate, is a reminder that it should be the privilege of every believer to experience the divine compassion *mediated through the fellowship of the church*. A cold and formal Christian community cannot hope to cope with the deprivation of spirit which leads to envy, jealousy and all manner of spiritual ills.

For some Christians, the very deepest healing has come through the realisation that the abyss of emptiness and loneliness has been traversed by Christ—at Calvary—and that they can meet Him just at that point where they face, perhaps for the first time, their own sense of forsakenness and inferiority. It is a frequent theme in psychoanalytic literature that healing comes when we reach the depths, but long before Freud the same truth recurred in religious writings. Jealousy is not overcome by telling ourselves how guilty we are. Rather, it is to be hoped that we can come at the right time to face that inner desolation and impoverishment that makes us feel perpetually inferior, and so envious of others who seem more blessed: to face it with Christ in whose presence the wilderness does rejoice and blossom as the rose.

Hatred—
 man against his neighbour

CHAPTER 6

Hatred—
man against his neighbour

There is at least one doctor who occasionally asks his patients the question, '*Who* is wrong with you?' Living or working in close proximity with someone for whom we have a deep antipathy is a frequent cause of nervous strain and tension. Of course, some might suggest that Christians should not have such feelings, or even that they do not have them. Yet few of us could claim that we have never entertained a strong and totally unjustified dislike for another person. And everyone who has tried to help people in difficulty knows of deeply sincere Christians thrown into despair because they feel violent hostility towards the mother-in-law who has come to share the home, or the colleague with whom they are in inescapable contact. The verdict of one of Sartre's characters, 'Hell is other people', certainly appears true in these situations.

People vary considerably in their ability to handle their feelings of aggression. Compelled to live or work with someone they find disagreeable, some insist on bringing the points of tension out into the open and, unpleasant as this may be, it is more likely to lead to a working compromise. Others bottle up their hostility, add to it a considerable amount of guilt, and then either allow the poison to undermine their health or wait for the pressures to build up towards one great explosion that shatters everyone around with its violence and unexpectedness.

Violent antipathy is not the only form that hatred takes. Censoriousness—the disposition to constant fault-finding, the urge to belittle every virtue and achievement—is as destructive in the long run, both to others and ourselves, as the more obvious hostility. Cynicism may be regarded as a hatred of life and therefore not to be considered under the heading of 'Man against his neighbour'. But the truth is that hatred of life always spills over into hatred of people. Resentment, too, is frequently tinged with animosity towards others.

For some people, enmity seems a necessary ingredient to life. In a short story by Somerset Maugham, two men who have been confined for years in a sanatorium spend their lives provoking one another, complaining about each other, and vieing with each for privileges. When one of them dies, however, the other is broken-hearted. Deprived of his enemy, he seems to have lost all purpose in living.

Anger is certainly a stimulant and we all tend to become more aggressive when we are tired or 'run down'. It may be that some people, by feeding their hostility towards those in their immediate environment, unconsciously attempt to solve what is basically a medical problem, or a problem caused by an over-crowded schedule. Writing about Edith Sitwell, the poet, with whom she worked closely for some years, Elizabeth Salter says, 'Crises were the order of the day, but she needed her crises as she needed her pests.' The ageing poet's 'pests' were the people who annoyed her, arousing the anger which helped to revive her flagging energy. Yet, as her biographer points out, this unnatural stimulation 'took its toll'.

To most of us for most of the time, however, feelings of hate and animosity are something we would very much rather do without. Life is sunnier and brighter when we feel at peace with our fellows and can co-operate with them without strain and tension. Perhaps we should remember this when we are tempted to condemn others for their hostility. Nobody *chooses* to feel like this, but most of us know what it is like to be overwhelmed by these emotions against our will.

To the Christian, these feelings of antipathy are not only

unpleasant but loaded with guilt. This can in turn intensify the hatred, for we naturally feel resentful towards those who appear to have robbed us of a good conscience.

How shall we deal with our hostilities? If the cause of our feelings is obvious—an unjust situation at work, the complete failure to recognise our needs in the family—then it is far better to talk this over with the people concerned than 'to suffer in silence'. We may imagine it is more Christian to forgo all our claims but serious consideration should be given to all aspects of the situation before we decide upon this course. For instance, if we refuse to complain but remain secretly resentful we will ultimately do far more damage than if we calmly air our disagreements. Again, the refusal to claim our rights, especially in the family, can have a very damaging effect on other members, particularly the children. A child who grows up in a family where Mum and Dad make it quite clear that they have rights which must be respected can happily claim his own rights. There is a form of 'self-sacrifice' which is harder to live with than any amount of self-assertion, because it carries an implied claim that everyone else should be equally self-sacrificing.

If our hostility towards others always had a rational cause how easy life would be! We would only need to choose our time wisely, make a reasonable approach, and more often than not difficult situations could be righted. But nine times out of ten we have to acknowledge that our antipathy is totally irrational. We just don't know why certain people arouse hostility in us, anymore than we know why we are so strongly drawn towards our friends. There are some people whose faults we cannot overlook and others of whose faults we are barely conscious, or indulgently excusing.

Obviously, the first step towards liberation is to try to find the cause of our hostility. This means being sufficiently honest, to begin with, to dismiss all those phoney 'reasons' which we have accumulated to justify our enmity.

At the root of a great deal of hatred lies that trick of the human mind whereby we project unacceptable parts of ourselves on to other people. We have already examined this process but it plays such an important part in our lives that the need to be aware of this should be reiterated. 'It is literally true,' claimed J.H. Hadfield, 'that in judging others we are trumpeting abroad our own secret faults. We personalise our unrecognised failings and hate in others the sins to which we are secretly addicted.'

Contrary to what most people imagine, the most virulent form of hatred is *self*-hatred. Our most intense animosity is directed towards that in other people which we dare not recognise in ourselves. This is the cause, not only of our more violent dislikes, but also of the prejudices that we have towards certain classes of people.

Hostility is also caused by the fact that others fail to meet the unrealistic and often unrecognised expectations we have of them. For instance, some people who had inadequate parents spend the rest of their lives unconsciously seeking for mother or father substitutes. As this expectation precludes an adult relationship, people with this problem find their relationships frequently disturbed and they experience intense hostility to those who they feel have 'let them down'.

It would be good to ask ourselves about anyone for whom we feel hostility, 'What am I wanting from him—or her? What deep expectations on my part are being denied?' We can then go on to ask whether these expectations are justified, or are they rather immature fantasies which still remain over from childhood.

David H. Fink tells the story of a father who was driven to the point of breakdown by the smothered hostility between himself and his son. The father had a fine intelligence but had been denied educational opportunities. Consequently his secret ambition to be a professional man was transferred to his son. Without being aware of what was happening, he cherished the hope of finding vicarious fulfilment through the boy's academic success. Unfortunately for him, the boy showed no interest in formal study. The father became increasingly hostile and the boy responded in kind. A sudden revelation of the depth of his anger towards his son was followed by an equally swift feeling of revulsion at the destructiveness of his own feelings. Repressing his anger, he succumbed to an acute anxiety state.

Hostility can sometimes be generated by the immature expectation which we entertain of some people that they be either faultless or omniscient. When we were children we managed to cope with the bewildering complexities of human nature by placing people in simple categories. There were the 'goodies' and the 'baddies'. An investigation into the effects of television upon children discovered that so long as 'the good' and 'the bad' are easily recognisable and *separate* children can tolerate considerable violence, death and other things that adults imagine would frighten them. What really alarms them is to find that the apparently 'good' is really villianous, the person one counted upon as being on one's side is actually an enemy.

Few of us entirely leave behind this over-simplified version of reality, but while we do not now categorise everyone we meet as a 'goody' or a 'baddy' *we still insist that some people shall fulfil our early expectations*. Consequently, people can get very angry if we try to prove to them that a violent criminal actually has some good in him, and they are even more angry when a clergyman, or the family doctor, fails to be the incarnation of goodness and knowledge. Here again we have unrealistic expectations leading to hostility.

We may trace the roots of our aggression still further if we recognise that we are all, in varying degrees, dependent upon some other people in our lives, and that dependence nearly always carries with it a certain amount of aggression. This can be experienced in the most loving relationship and it does not mean that we secretly hate those we think we love. We become aggressive in order to maintain the difference between ourselves and those upon whom we might become over-dependent. Without our being aware of what is happening, our personalities are saying no to the identity which is the death of individuality, and yes to true relationship, which includes difference as well as similarity.

Unhappy experiences of long ago, which we have pushed down into the unconscious levels of the mind, sometimes predispose us to suspect and dislike anyone whose role or personality remotely resembles those of the people who once made us afraid and unhappy.

We see, then, that hostility has its roots more often in ourselves than in the exterior situation. We hate in others what we refuse to see in ourselves; we resent people not fulfilling the expectations we unconsciously cherish of them; we sometimes feel aggressive towards those upon whom we greatly depend and we dislike those who touch the chords of long-forgotten and unhappy experiences.

Obviously, we shall not always be able to work through to an understanding of the causes of our antipathy, though it is always worth trying to do this. When we cannot understand our dislikes, it will be a triumph of Christian charity if we refuse to rationalise them and bear our feelings with regret, continuing to hope that we may eventually see the other with fresh eyes and genuine appreciation.

Certainly the Christian cannot be content to remain in a state of hostility towards another, though it is equally true that he cannot just lift himself out of this simply by an act of will. In different situations different tactics are called for. For instance, our dislike for someone we hardly ever speak to will often be dissipated by taking the trouble to get to know them better, and it is surely a Christian duty to take this trouble. Praying for a person towards whom we feel hostile will invariably help us to see them in a different light.

Throughout the whole of this chapter we have been considering the hostility and antipathy we feel towards particular people. There is, however, an even more unhappy condition which was mentioned briefly—that is the hatred of life itself which always spills over into our relationships. The causes of such hatred are myriad: early deprivation of love, continual disappointment and frustration, personal moral failure, betrayal by those we trusted. Usually it is the accumulated effect of many such blows that makes a man a cynic, or one who hates life itself.

Few can drag themselves out of this miry pit, for more than a few faulty attitudes towards individual people are entailed. The whole orientation of life is askew and for the correction of this we need the sympathetic understanding and insight of another.

It is surprising how one wholesome relationship, or even an engrossing interest, can become the bridgehead of healing forces in a personality. Nobody 'in love' was ever capable of total cynicism, and the truly creative person is always less prone to react to injury with destructive malice. The cynic desperately needs a friendship or a responsibility which draws out those positive, but at present latent, emotions which are life-affirming instead of life-negating. This means that he cannot heal himself, which is another way of stating the Christian doctrine that we are saved by grace.

Undoubtedly, the direction of a life can be diverted from destructiveness, malice and cynicism towards creativity, co-operation and hope by what is an obviously religious experience. What better grounds can there possibly be for this glad transformation than the discovery of a Love that is utterly reliable, ceaselessly active and ultimately triumphant? It may also happen that a good friend who sees beneath the bitterness to the hidden and often unacknowledged wounds can also bring healing and release. And since human love is a pale reflection of the divine compassion this redemptive experience is surely no less religious.

Certainly the Christian knows that, if he is to practise what he believes, he must view his antipathy and even his hatred in the light of the Cross of Christ where unrelenting malice was conquered by unlimited love. At times, he must just suffer, in deep humiliation, the fact that his feelings are so alien to his calling, though never without a prayer that the love of Christ may dissolve his antagonisms, and never without renewing his resolve that he will not falsely seek to justify his feelings by blaming his 'enemy' instead of patiently seeking for the reasons in himself.

The Promise and Perils
of Self-Awareness

CHAPTER 7

The Promise and Perils of Self-Awareness

Martin Buber, the Jewish philosopher, recounted a dream in which he stood before the Judgement Seat awaiting a verdict on his life. Thunderous words issued forth: 'Martin Buber, I ask you not, "Why were you not Moses?" "Why were you not Rabbi Baal Shem Tove?" I ask you only, "Why were you not Martin Buber?" '

Trying to emulate other people, rather than fulfilling our own possibilities to the full, is a temptation to which we all at times succumb. Yet if we are to become our true selves we must heed the ancient wisdom that has been handed down to us from the earliest period of philosophy: 'Know thyself'.

It has been an axiom of most schools of psychotherapy that gaining insight into the way our personalities work helps to diminish neurotic symptoms and prepares the way for personal growth. As we shall see later, self-understanding is not always sufficient in itself to bring healing, nor is the path to self-knowledge without dangers. It is interesting to note, however, that masters of the spiritual life have usually made the same assumption that progress requires insight into ourselves, no matter how painful and disquieting this may be.

John Nicholas Grou, an eighteenth-century Jesuit priest, claimed that as soon as God is 'certain of a man, immediately He begins to enlighten him as to his defects; He raises by degrees the veil which concealed them from him, and He inspires him with a firm will to overcome them . . . God shows him all this gradually; for if He were to show it to him all at once he could not bear it, and would fall into despair.'

Turning from catholic to protestant spirituality we find this same insistence that the way forward is through the travail of self-discovery. After conversion, wrote John Wesley, believers enjoy their new-found peace 'for days, or weeks, or months, and commonly suppose that they shall not know war any more; till some of their old enemies, their bosom sins, or the sin which did most easily beset them (perhaps anger or desire), assault them again, and thrust sore at them that they may fall . . . Under these clouds, especially if they reasoned with the devil, they go mourning all the day long. But it is seldom long before their Lord answers for Himself, sending them the Holy Ghost to comfort them, to bear witness continually with their spirits that they are the children of God. Then they are indeed meek, and gentle, and teachable, even as little children; and now do they see the ground of their heart, which God before would not disclose unto them, lest the soul should fail before Him and the spirit which He had made. Now they see all the hidden abomination there, the depths of pride, self-will and hell.'

When ancient wisdom, modern psychotherapy and Christian spirituality agree on the importance of knowing ourselves, we can surely dismiss the contrary view, embodied in a letter to *The Daily Express* on the subject of depth psychology, that 'sane, clean-living folk do not concern themselves with what may or may not go on inside their heads.'

Self-knowledge is essential if we are to realise our full potentialities. That we may stifle a valuable part of our personality in the interests of tame conformity is the possibility envisaged in Dante Gabriel Rossetti's poem *The Murdered Selves*:

> I do not see them here: but after death
> God knows, I know the faces I shall see,
> Each one a murdered self, with low, last breath.
> 'I am thyself,—What hast thou done to me?'
> 'And I—and I—thyself,' (lo, each one saith),
> 'And thou thyself to all eternity!'

In this chapter, however, we are concerned with self-knowledge, not primarily as a requisite to full development of the personality, but as one way in which our rebel emotions are understood and harnessed. How does self-knowledge diminish anxiety, depression and the other distressing symptoms we have so far considered?

In so far as anxiety is often a state of over-alertness, in which the mind guards against memories, feelings and desires which it cannot admit to consciousness, it is obvious that every gain in self-awareness is bound to lower the level of tension. A character in T. S. Eliot's play *The Elder Statesman* refers to 'the man who in the morning has to make up his face before he looks into the mirror'. To be as deceived as this about one's true nature, to be so alienated from one's own depths, is necessarily to live in a state of eternal vigilance. The lie detector machine is built upon the assumption that every deception raises somewhat the level of anxiety. It is not always recognised that self-deception has the same result, though it must be added that most self-deception is unconscious and therefore not blameworthy. Often we just dare not acknowledge the truth about ourselves.

Many of our emotional problems are due to our difficulties in relating to other people. Here we encounter the kind of vicious circle which is so prominent a feature of nervous suffering. The tense, shy or over-aggressive person fails to make friends or creates hostility and this serves to increase his anxiety or depression. He becomes more solitary, so his emotional problems are intensified. How does growth in self-awareness improve our capacity to make good relationships?

First, as we become more aware of the parts of our personalities which we have repudiated we cease to project these on to other people. Had the Pharisees in the gospel story been healthily in touch with their own sexuality they would not have been so censorious and vindictive in their attitude to the woman taken in adultery. It was when Jesus reminded them of their own failures that their zeal to see punishment meted out began to wane.

When we refuse to recognise conflict in ourselves the same conflict is nearly always displaced into the outer world where it can be fought out with other people. When we acknowledge the conflict in ourselves, our own relationships improve. E. N. Ducker writes: 'Although psychologists are as various as Christians in their opinions, they are agreed in one matter: which is, that the problem of any "one" is to relate himself to his "duality", by living through the stress of this relationship with his alien, unfriendly and apparently destructive "other". If I can live with my other self, I can more easily bear to live with you. But if I hate myself, I shall certainly hate you. As Shakespeare said: "Love, loving not itself, none other can." From this derives the practice of all effective psychotherapy.'

Understanding ourselves also helps us to recognise how our expectations of others may be formulated by our own problems and be to that extent unrealistic. The persons who did not receive the parental affection they needed in childhood may go all their life unconsciously seeking mother or father substitutes and, since few people are prepared to play this role, one friendship after another breaks down. The projection of infantile hopes upon husband or wife is a frequent source of marital disharmony. We all regress at times in our relationships. There are few husbands who do not welcome a little mothering from their wives while they battle with a bout of flu. But when the regression is more or less permanent the adult in each partner is left unsatisfied.

Self-awareness frees our relationships from the distorting effects of our own unconscious fears and expectations. The more we are in touch with our own depths the more we can be deeply in touch with other people.

* * *

How is self-knowledge gained? Margaret Isherwood describes a young woman who, when asked why she was trying to escape from herself, replied: 'Myself, I've not the foggiest notion who or what that is. Maybe if I go a long way off into a different kind of environment, another world, I'll find out who I am, or whether I'm really anybody at all, or just a series of events in time . . . a psycho-physical process.'

It is a common illusion that we could discover our true selves in some other environment, but the truth is that all the barriers to self-knowledge are in ourselves. This means that our quest is one of the most difficult we can undertake for, in effect, we have to begin a game of hide and seek with ourselves. This means that the more concentrated our self-examination the more subtle becomes our self-evasion. Growth in understanding ourselves comes more from the ability to catch ourselves out than by placing ourselves under a microscope. Being rigorously honest about our reactions, refusing to call our cowardice prudence, or our rashness courage: this is the way to self-awareness.

We all know what it is to react to certain situations or people in an exaggerated way, and this is an indication that a rather sensitive area of our personalities is being probed. In particular, we can learn a lot about ourselves from the people we specially dislike. Frequently we become hostile to that in others which reminds us of a part of ourselves we have repudiated. Similarly, we become most incensed about the sins in others we would secretly like to commit. We do, of course, become angry about the hurts inflicted upon others. But, with this exception, the reaction of the good person to the wrongdoing he observes is usually one of grief and sorrow.

Psychoanalysis has always stressed the importance of dreams in self-understanding and Freud claimed they were the royal road to the unconscious. The interpretation of dreams requires considerable training, skill and an intimate knowledge of the dreamer. But we can all learn to know ourselves better through our day-dreams (always supposing the rush of modern life leaves time for this useful activity) and from the occasional dream which is less complex than usual. Frequently, after a conversation with someone, we will ourselves re-enact the episode in our imaginations but with certain revisions. Those revisions can be very revealing. Similarly, the man who never argues with his boss, or disagrees with his wife, may dream that he is telling them what he thinks in a most aggressive and violent manner. It is the part of ourselves we do not normally admit to consciousness, let alone allow expression in action, that slips past the inner censor into our dreams and fantasies.

* * *

Like all worthwhile tasks the quest for self-understanding is beset by perils. It is these dangers that lead to the wholesale condemnation of every attempt to know ourselves as 'morbid introspection'. To become totally absorbed in oneself *is* morbid: it is also self-defeating. We understand ourselves best in relationship with others and the more absorbed we become with ourselves the more unrelated we become.

The road to self-knowledge must be trod with great patience and in recognition that few arrive at the goal in this life. If we could glimpse the whole truth in an instant we should be shattered by it, or alternatively quite unable to assimilate it. Therefore we must be well satisfied if we are making slow but steady progress. 'I sometimes pray', wrote C. S. Lewis, 'not for self-knowledge in general but for just so much self-knowledge at the moment as I can bear and use at the moment; the little daily dose.' If it is helpful to cultivate a gentle watchfulness over what is going on within us, it is equally necessary to cultivate every interest in the outer world of people and events.

A very real danger attending the search for self-knowledge is that we may come to *identify* ourselves with what Carl Jung called 'the shadow'—that part of ourselves which we have repressed because it is inconsistent with the values of the society in which we live. 'The individual is driven by his personal crisis', writes Eric Neumann, 'into deep waters which he would usually never have entered if left to his own free will. The old idealised image of the ego has to go, and its place is taken by a perilous insight into the ambiguity and many-sidedness of one's own nature.'

We need to remember, however, that if the old idealised image of ourselves was not the whole truth, neither are the tempestuous instinctive forces, the newly-discovered hostilities and the pervasive self-interest the whole truth. Towards the shadow aspect of our personalities we must adopt a finely balanced attitude: neither denying its existence nor attributing to it total importance.

A person who has not previously subjected himself to close scrutiny, and who starts on the task of self-understanding because of some personal crisis or breakdown, frequently becomes alarmed by what he discovers. In Iris Murdoch's novel *The Nice and the Good* two youngsters, Pierce and Barbara, are talking together. 'When I was younger,' says Barbara, 'when I read in the papers and in books and things about really nasty people, bad people, I felt that these people were just utterly different from me, that I could never become bad or behave really bad like them. Did you feel this?' 'I don't know,' replies Pierce; 'I think boys always know about badness.' 'Well,' says Barbara, 'I'm afraid it's all turning out to be much more difficult than I expected.'

The process of disillusionment about ourselves, so essential if we are ever to build our characters on a surer foundation, is usually deeply discouraging. It is just at this point that the Christian may find in his faith the strength and comfort he needs. Nobody saw more clearly into the heart of men and women than Christ, yet on every page of the gospels His deep compassion for them is manifest. If, as Christians believe,

God is like Jesus, the believer has more grounds than the unbeliever for being able to face the very worst in himself without ultimate despair. God knows us, loves us and is at work in our lives to turn the dross of our characters into pure gold.

One of the best contemporary illustrations of the quest for self-knowledge is found in *Markings*, the journal of Dag Hammarskjöld, one-time Secretary General of the United Nations Organisation. The rigorous honesty of this brilliant, sensitive man, as he probes his own motives and confronts his fears, makes poignant reading. At times, he seems to be on the brink of despair, but his faith in God never wavers and it is this that provides a rock of security beneath his feet. In one entry he wrote, 'It is when we stand in the righteous all-seeing light of love that we can dare to look at, admit and consciously suffer under this something in us which wills disaster, misfortune, defeat to everything outside the sphere of our narrowest self-interest. So a living relation to God is the necessary pre-condition for the self-knowledge which enables us to follow a straight path, and so be victorious over ourselves, forgiven by ourselves!'

Finally, we must remember that insight into ourselves, though immensely valuable, will not solve all problems. Some schools of psychotherapy have made understanding of the origin of our problems the sole goal, believing that once blockages to growth are removed the sufferer will move towards maturity. These therapists trust the innate healthiness of the mind to complete the work they begin.

This would seem a proper recognition of the limits of psychotherapy, for it is not the task of the doctor or counsellor to impose his own philosophy or life-goals upon the person who comes to him for help. It must be recognised, however, that freeing ourselves from the influence of past wounds, or correcting faulty patterns of reaction, is not enough to provide a healthy, satisfying life. Understanding ourselves is important: it is not all-important.

'We must love one another
or die'

CHAPTER 8

'We must love one another or die'

It will not have passed unnoticed that all the 'rebel emotions' considered so far have their origins in disturbed personal relationships, perhaps in earliest childhood, and in turn they tend to create havoc in our present relationships. If destructive emotions are to be dissolved a person needs to gain insight into and understanding of himself, but this is only a part of the answer. We do not want and cannot have an emotional void, with hatred, lust and jealousy forever banished: we rather desire a healthily functioning personality in which creative and positive emotions are dominant. In the end, we are healed only when good relationships have replaced relationships marked by fear, dependency hatred and exploitation. Our real need is for love.

The title for this chapter is taken from the poem, *September 1st 1939*, by W. H. Auden. It is true politically, for unless modern man finds the way to harmonious international relationships he may well destroy himself. It is true biologically, for at that simple level man needs to reproduce himself or the species would die out. They are also true personally, for a loveless life is a warped, frustrated and eventually a destructive life.

In the novel by the Israeli novelist Shin Shalom, *Storm Over Galilee*, a group of children are gathered on the roof of their school, as they did every week, taking it in turns to look at the stars through an ancient telescope. Many exclamations of awe and wonder pass their lips, but one girl makes the same comment on every occasion. 'Teacher, I want to be a star; I ever so much want to be a star!' 'Why, child?' the teacher asks. 'Because they are lucky, those stars are ever so lucky.' 'What makes you think so, child?' is the next question. 'Because teacher loves those stars', comes the reply.

Few adults can dare to make even that sort of shy admission of our hunger for love. Yet deep down we do believe that love is the answer to our difficulties. It is highly significant, however, that more people see this in terms of a hunger to receive love than in the need to give love. Of course, we all require to feel appreciated and wanted. Our hunger for love is perfectly legitimate. All too often, however, our long and weary search for people who will love us is a subtle and necessary piece of self-deception. Necessary because it is ultimately easier to complain, 'Nobody loves me', than to admit, 'I am incapable of loving'. The recognition of the lovelessness of our own personalities, of the icy coldness inside us, is an anguish that few have the courage to face.

The pain of the person who feels incapable of returning love is well described in a poem by Edward Thomas, *No One So Much as You*.

> No one so much as you
> Loves this my clay,
> Or would lament as you
> Its dying day.

Here then is absolute assurance of *being* loved, but also with this the anguish of being unable to return love.

> My eyes scarce dare meet you
> Lest they should prove
> I but respond to you
> And do not love.

What the poet describes about one particular relationship some people feel about all relationships. If it is true that 'we must love one another or die' this plight might well appear a comparatively hopeless one. Is there a creative way of facing even this affliction?

Nothing is to be gained by fostering either guilt or inferiority. The person who is afraid of loving, who panics at the thought of close relationships, has at some time passed through an experience in which loving became inextricably bound up with pain. In the deep places of his personality, and without any conscious decision on his part, he once came to the awful conclusion, 'To love is to be hurt; to be hurt so deeply that this is a vulnerability I cannot afford.' As this was not a conscious decision guilt is irrelevant, and as he had as much capacity for loving as the next before the psychic catastrophe which made love so painful, there are equally no rational grounds for inferiority.

Being able to love is just one aspect of being a mature person. Every step we take in self-knowledge and towards personal maturity increases our chances of becoming loving people. But we cannot just sit back and wait for this to happen. There is an important truth in the advice which Florence Allshorn used to give about exercising our capacity for love, however small that may be. 'It's worth conquering all along the line,' she wrote in a letter to a friend, 'attitudes of positive love always in every tiny thing. Practise, practise, practise as you would if you were Paderewski.'

It is at this point that some would wish to make a sharp distinction between 'love' and 'Christian love'. The latter, as they argue, is an attitude of the will, not a state of the emotions. It is therefore possible, and indeed necessary, to offer 'Christian love' even to people we do not like. There is, of course, an important truth here. We cannot wait on our feelings of compassion before we act compassionately; we dare not delay until feelings of animosity have disappeared before we seek to be reconciled to our 'enemy'. The right feelings can follow the right actions as well as be the dynamic which inspires them.

What is surely important is that our 'Christian love' is

never regarded as an evasion of the need to find what is likeable in the other person, that it should always be open to the possibility that it will not remain only an act of will. If someone is gritting his teeth to exhibit 'Christian love' towards me, at the same time having decided *once for all* that I am a thoroughly unlikeable person, I feel inclined to tell him he need not bother.

The love which is only a matter of the will must surely be seen as a temporary solution, a going out to the other person with an implied hope and prayer that genuine appreciation and its associated emotions will follow.

In so far as we find it hard to love we should inquire into the deficiencies in our love for ourselves. Despite a long and pernicious religious tradition teaching that love for oneself is the root of all sin, there has been an equally long and more healthy tradition, including the teaching of Jesus Himself, which asserts the necessity of loving oneself. 'Love your neighbour as yourself' is the soundest psychology as well as the highest ethic. Meister Eckhart, the thirteenth-century mystic, wrote, 'If you love yourself, you love everybody else as you do yourself. As long as you love another person less than you love yourself, you will not really succeed in loving yourself, but if you love all alike, including yourself, you will love them as one person and that person is both God and man. Thus he is a great and righteous person who, loving himself, loves all others equally.'

If we have had any experience at all of helping people with emotional difficulties we will have noticed repeatedly that those who hate themselves also despise others, and those who love others know how to appreciate and value themselves. We lack love for our fellows, not because we squander it upon ourselves, but because the same fear that inhibits our self-giving makes us defensively selfish, and selfishness is a very different thing from proper self-love.

To increase our capacity for loving we also need courage to recognise that what we often regard as affection for others falls far short of true love. In human relationships appearances are often deceptive, though I suspect that very deep down most of us know more of the truth than we dare to admit. That we desperately need another person is no guarantee that we love them: perhaps we need them for reassurance, or as a child needs a parent, or in order to exploit, or as a desperate remedy against loneliness. Most of our loving is imperfect and some of what looks like love is nothing less than disguised egotism. We need to see this *and not despair*. Otherwise we may spend our whole lives imagining that we truly love when in fact we merely use people to meet our needs.

If we have become alienated from our emotions, and so find it difficult to feel loving, we should have a great deal of patience with ourselves. To confront our own lovelessness is far harder than to accept that we are unloved. Patient endurance and trust in God can turn even this affliction into ultimate gain. Simone Weil claimed that extreme affliction is rather as though the point of a nail were applied to the very centre of a human soul, and the whole shock received by the large head of the nail passes to that one point. 'The man to whom such a thing happens has no part in the operation,' she wrote. 'He struggles like a butterfly which is pinned alive into an album. But through all the horror he can continue to *want* to love. There is nothing impossible in that, no obstacle, one might almost say no difficulty. For the greatest suffering . . . does not touch the part of the soul which consents to a right direction. It is only necessary to know that love is a direction and not a state of the soul.'

Patient acceptance of our own fear of loving also requires that we forgo anxious testing of our feelings to see whether any improvement is taking place. Loving *feelings* are much more likely to creep up upon us unawares while we steadily get on with the business of *acting* with concern, respect and consideration for others.

The capacity to love is always comprehensive in scope. We

need to recognise this both in order to gain some realistic assessment of how loving we are, and in order to enlarge the faculty we possess. Many people who are basically unloving deceive themselves into thinking that the very strong feelings they have towards a few individuals marks them out as loving people or, alternatively, they imagine that if only the right person would come along the miracle would happen. They are great lovers whom the universe has cheated by failing to unite their path with the paths of those with whom they would, quite effortlessly, have found bliss.

Love is a faculty which, if it is developed at all, will operate, though in varying degrees, in *every* relationship. Sebastian Moore quotes the axiom which one sophisticated French woman handed on to young ladies: 'If you want the men to love you, be kind and thoughtful to old ladies.' He adds, 'Maybe she was beginning to feel the draught herself and could do with a bit of attention! Anyhow, what she says is true.'

This idea of the essential comprehensiveness of love is one of the major themes in Erich Fromm's book *The Art of Loving*. He claims that objectivity—the ability to see the other person undistorted by our own desires, hopes and fears—is an important element in loving, and then adds, 'But it must be acquired with regard to everybody with whom one comes in contact. If someone would want to reserve his objectivity for the loved person, and think he can dispense with it in his relationship to the rest of the world, he will soon discover that he fails both here and there.'

Judging by this standard some of us may be forced to the conclusion that we are less loving than we imagined. But there is also a hopeful aspect; if love is a comprehensive faculty we can begin to develop it at any time and in any place. We do not have to wait for the person with whom we feel a natural affinity, we can practise the art of loving in far less promising situations with those who bore and infuriate us. And we cannot develop our capacity for love within the circle of our family and friends without ultimately having something more to offer to every person we meet. Similarly, we cannot restrict our loving to a few without eventually having less to offer even to those so favoured.

For the Christian, love is not only an aspect of human relationships. He recognises with the psychologists that *being* loved precedes loving, that the unloved child will find it infinitely harder to love. But he also believes in a divine love which far transcends, and is also the source of, human compassion. 'We love because He first loved us' (1 John 4:19, N.E.B.). Every religious practice—whether it be prayer, Bible reading or Christian fellowship—which makes real to us the love of God, is a means whereby we may overcome our fear of loving. And every experience of human love is seen to be an experience of divine grace.

Does Prayer help?

CHAPTER 9

Does Prayer help?

Perhaps the best known of all modern criticisms of religion is Freud's assertion that it is the universal neurosis of mankind. He interpreted prayer and worship as psychological projections which not only express emotional immaturity but also serve to keep believers immature. To Freud, God was a father-substitute, necessary only to those who fail to grow up and attain adult independence.

Christianity has proved itself most virile when able to learn from its critics, and this is true with this particular objection to Christian faith. That there are elements of truth in Freud's assertion few Christian psychiatrists would deny. All too often people use religion to serve infantile desires which should instead be outgrown. Their religion then becomes a positive hindrance to emotional development.

This misuse of religion is no valid reason for its abandonment. We would expect that emotional disturbance will distort our religious experience just as it distorts, in varying degrees, our human relationships. What we urgently need is an understanding of the ways in which this occurs. Just as we recognise some patterns of human conduct as neurotic so we should be able to tell when religious experience is disturbed by deep fears and insecurities. Moreover, we must discover what kind of religion facilitates emotional growth and what kind impedes such development. This is a crucial question for the church at large but it is particularly urgent for the sufferer from nervous illness.

When we ask: Does prayer help? we are concerned with much more than how we use certain periods of time set apart for devotional exercises, helpful though these are. In deep depression or acute anxiety a person may have to limit or even abandon such practices. He will not on this account cease to pray, but simply maintain his relationship with God in other ways, perhaps by brief acts of self-surrender and committal, by repeated affirmations of that divine presence which he is quite incapable of feeling.

In this chapter we look at certain key issues which play an important part in determining whether or not our religion facilitates healing and emotional growth. First, what images of God do we use and how do we see our relationship to Him? Second, what 'model' of Christian life do we hold and does this enable us to handle our guilt and achieve self-understanding? Third, does our prayer and worship engage the whole personality, or does it remain only emotional, or only intellectual?

* * *

In a *Punch* cartoon some explorers were being met by a missionary dressed, incredibly, in a dog-collar, black coat and trousers, wringing his hands and saying, 'I'm afraid there has been a terrible mistake.' The reason for his consternation was depicted in the background. A tribal dance was in full swing round a totem pole carved to portray a man in dog-collar, black coat and trousers.

The tendency to create God in our image extends, in the Christian religion, even to Christ. One would have thought that, having actual records of the life of Jesus, Christians would have been less prone to distort His image. Yet it is surprising how much the church's thinking of Jesus has always been influenced by the conditions of the time. During the Constantine Empire, for example, artists portrayed Him as Pantocreator, or Ruler of the universe, in huge mosaics on church ceilings. As the empire weakened pictures of Jesus became less regal, more human. In one era artists and theologians concentrated almost exclusively upon the suffering of Jesus. At other times He was presented as a Judge so austere that only devotion to Mary, His mother, by providing an essential element of tenderness, saved the faith from becoming a crushing and intolerable burden.

William Blake clearly saw how believers may mean very different things even when they use precisely the same language.

> The vision of Christ that thou dost see
> Is my vision's greatest enemy . . .
> Thine loves the same things that mine hates,
> Thy heaven's doors are my hell's gates.

In talking to people burdened by nervous suffering one repeatedly finds that they labour under an image of God which, if applied to a fellow human being, would constitute him the most unattractive person imaginable. This image is often an amalgam of the more primitive parts of the Old Testament together with the less pleasant emotions aroused in the person's earliest experience with his own parents.

Almost as damaging to spiritual and emotional development is the image of God which is *only* an embodiment of pleasant childhood experience. This can too easily lead to a religious experience which is nothing more than the satisfaction of infantile wishes.

Obviously our image of God must greatly influence our religious experience, yet few believers subject this image to close scrutiny. Moreover, it is surprising how little our feelings about God are affected by theological concepts. We may have attained considerable sophistication in our conscious thinking about God, yet maintain essentially infantile feelings towards Him. This is because our image is composed of unconscious as well as conscious elements.

We need to heed the warning of Lord Eccles when he writes: 'The experience of art shows that whatever man may do with facts he cannot play fast and loose with images. We look at Turner's sunsets in the Tate Gallery and cannot again look at a natural sunset in the same way. What kind of image then is likely to enrich our knowledge of that love which . . . God is?'

An inadequate image of God is not in itself dangerous, for the most soaring vision of the mystic falls short of the divine reality. What is dangerous is the rigid, fixed image of God which makes impossible further growth of understanding. Just as the growing child constantly modifies and changes his picture of his parents until eventually a totally different relationship is achieved, so the believer should be revising and enlarging his understanding of God. If this is not happening, if we think about and respond to God just as we have always done, it means our concepts are being petrified by some neurotic defence. We are clinging to fantasies, not to God Himself. 'Wrong prayer, like a bad diet, can have serious consequences,' writes R. S. Lee. 'When we are confident we know the absolute truth of God, confident to the degree of dogmatism, our prayers become drugs to take away our power to respond to life, that is, to God. Instead of promoting growth they arrest it.'

In the Bible, an abundant wealth of imagery is used in speaking about God. He is King, Shepherd, Husband, Father, Rock, Shield and Spirit. No single image is literally true or fully adequate to convey the whole truth about God. We need to remember the inviolable mystery which always surrounds the divine and to keep our thinking about God open-ended. The only fixed point in our understanding of God is that He is most fully revealed in Christ. Nothing can be true of Him which does not harmonise with Calvary.

If prayer is to a God who is but the projection of infantile hopes and fears it will serve to keep us immature: if prayer means opening ourselves to reality, being willing to abandon cherished notions and learn from experience, then it will assist development.

Closely linked with the image, or images, we hold of God

is the type of relationship we seek to establish towards Him. Religion has often been described in terms of a sense of dependence. It makes all the difference in the world how this dependence is envisaged. The helpless baby at his mother's breast is a perfect picture of total dependence but God does not encourage us to remain in this stage of passivity.

There is a dependence which imprisons a person in immaturity, saving him from the need to develop his own powers of discrimination, blocking his progress towards self-confidence. Psychiatrists tell us that such dependence is always accompanied by deep resentment, for to be kept in a state of dependence is to be deprived of our adult status.

Earl Loomis reminds us that the urge towards independence is essential to development. 'We're all familiar with the child who says, "I won't", when you tell him to brush his teeth, and then proceeds to brush them surreptitiously, as if to say, "Dad, that's your idea. When I brush my teeth it's going to be my idea." But in this gesture of defiance the child affirms both the father's reality as a person and his own reality as a separate self.'

The difficulty with the father-child image of man's relationship with God is that it may be taken at either end of what is a rapidly changing relationship, from total, unquestioning dependence, to adult companionship and partnership. On the human level, the better the relationship between father and son the easier it is for the child to grow up within that relationship. It is poor fathering that keeps a child immature or forces it into total rebellion. Yet some forms of religion seem to offer believers only these two options.

In the New Testament the figure of 'sonship' stands for a mature relationship with God the Father. The 'son' enters into the father's plans and projects in a way the servant cannot. Sonship means the acceptance of responsibility and is nearer to the idea of being 'workers together with God' than to the total dependence of early childhood.

Harvey Cox claims that recent discussions on the concept of covenant in the Old Testament suggest that it meant that God was willing to stoop so low as to work in tandem with man, to work on a team, no matter how poorly the human partner was working out . . . It is not demeaning to suggest that the notions of teamwork and partnership need to be explored much more in our conceptualisation of God. He who is "high and lifted up" suggests in the life of Jesus that He is willing to put Himself in the position of working within a group, of washing His fellows' feet and of needing someone to carry His cross. What seems at first sight irreverence may be closer to the heart of the self-humbling truth of God than we imagine.'

We have repeatedly noted in this book that emotional problems stem from a failure to outgrow infantile fears and conflicts. Before we can confidently answer the question 'Does prayer help?' we need to be clear about the kind of relationship to God we are seeking. That we are utterly dependent upon God for our very existence goes without saying. Yet the Bible clearly suggests that, within this dependent relationship, man should attain maturity and accept and our relationship to Him are important: so is the view we have of presence continually upon us. He wants full-grown sons and daughters, not retarded infants.

*   *   *

Whether prayer assists us to know ourselves better, and so to become more free of neurotic symptoms, or whether it merely strengthens repression and so impedes progress, will also depend upon the 'model' of the Christian life we place before us. Our view of God and our relationship to Him are important: so is the view we have of Christian discipleship. For instance, if we imagine that surrender to God results in instant perfection we shall, of course, violently resist any insight that shows how far we are from the goal. Our religion, including our prayer life, will aim at outward conformity and seek to evade confronting our own depths. The result is the kind of superficiality which fools nobody but ourselves. Is our view of the Christian life one of faultless behaviour, requiring mostly the successful denial of our more unacceptable feelings, or is it one of growing self-awareness and integration?

A number of different models of Christian discipleship have succeeded each other through the ages. It is easy to be wise after the event and see the deficiencies of, say, the kind of spirituality which required total withdrawal from the life of men in order to devote oneself wholly to God, or that which was wholly devoted to saving men's souls, but void of social concern. Yet these models of discipleship seemed valid at the time and a correct historical perspective would allow us to appreciate them as ways in which, in particular eras, men responded to God's love.

Does our greater understanding of human personality now require from us a somewhat modified 'model' of Christian living, one more concerned with inner growth towards maturity and less preoccupied with particular sins? If so, then our whole approach to confessional prayer must be changed.

Confession of sin has always played a prominent part in prayer and worship. Traditionally it has been regarded as necessary to that cleansing without which it is impossible to gain a clearer vision of God. Yet confession that lingers too long upon what we have done or failed to do is largely unproductive and tends to become morbid. Having acknowledged failure and accepted God's forgiveness, we need to turn our attention to what can be done now and in the future. It is a good practice to refuse to confess any particular sinful action more than once. After all, to ask for God's pardon repeatedly for the same offence is an implicit denial of His promise that if we confess our sins He is faithful and just to forgive us our sins (1 John 1:9).

Having received God's pardon we can usefully consider what we have done and what we have omitted to do only as an indication of *what we are*. This means laying bare before God, not only the attitudes and feelings we now renounce but those we still find it impossible to surrender. Too often prayer consists of telling God only what we think He would like to hear. This hardly promotes self-knowledge.

Many religious people hesitate to express verbally, and before God, their doubts, antagonisms, and worldly ambitions. Yet to do so is often to bring a new note of reality into our relationship with God. We are not asking for His approval of our dubious desires: we are holding them up in His presence so as to come to a new assessment of them and be able to renounce what conflicts with God's will. But the bold, scrupulously honest declaration of our real desires may well be necessary before we progress to the place where we desire what God wants.

One of the rather quaint characters who appear in Bernard Bassett's book *We Neurotics* is describing a method of confessional prayer which aims at self-discovery, not just release from the burden of guilt. She suggests to another character that he first adopt a completely relaxed position and then start the thrilling journey to the centre of the soul. 'Let me put it this way,' she says. 'Do you know those little cardboard models of the human body used by doctors and nurses in their student days? You have a flat little cardboard man with no clothes on so that the students may study his superficial structure, skin, joints and veins. You put the little fellow flat on his back and you open up his first little flaps. Up with the skin and the ribs and you come to the various organs, starting with the lungs. Up with the lungs and you come to the heart, up with the heart and you find the liver, up with the liver and all the tubing and eventually you come to his spine. Admittedly it is not very elegant but that is how I pray. I open myself up layer by layer, starting with myself on the surface . . . Next I come down to myself in my room when no one is looking, my games, my fears, my vanity, the fact that I never married, my sorrow, my remorse. Open that up and I arrive at the Ego or what I would prefer to call the heart . . . I sit or lie down and . . . I say inside, "Take a peep, O Lord".'

This way of describing confessional prayer may or may not appeal to us, but the aim is sound. Recounting failures too often leaves us just where we were before, except that we feel less uncomfortable now that we have 'owned up'. Much more is required if we are genuinely to grow in grace.

*   *   *

Another test to which we should subject our prayer and worship is to ask whether it engages the whole person—intellect, emotion and will. Many of us suffer from some degree of one-sidedness and this will reveal itself in our religious practice. We may have an alert intellect but impoverished emotions, or lively emotions and a lazy mind. Unfortunately we are drawn to those parts of the Christian church, and to those forms of devotion, which cater for our strength but ignore our weakness. To some people, religion is a perpetual debate, to others an emotional orgy.

Progress towards maturity means recognising where our development is somewhat retarded and cultivating what we have previously neglected. Gilbert Russell, a Christian psychotherapist, writes, 'A professional man of fifty, intellectually able, conscientious to a fault, but in despair about his relationship with his wife, tried to commit suicide. He dreamed when he came to analysis that he was leaving the bookshop where he had worked for years and "returning" to Kew Gardens where (it seemed in his dream) he was employed as a boy. His completely one-sided development had left him high and dry, without a single human contact of any significance. He had to turn from the intellectual approach to life in which he was petrified, and go back to the place where things could be made to grow.'

Ideally, the worship of God includes the ceaseless quest for truth which engages the intellect, the response of the emotions to the approach of the divine Lover, the dedication of the will to the purposes of God. It does not require great insight to know which aspect of our personality plays little part in our religious life and then gently to nurture it. Of course, one person's approach to life will always be predominantly emotional, while another person's is mainly intellectual. It is only when one aspect is developed at the expense of the other that real impoverishment results.

Prayer does help us to become more mature to the extent that it means relating our whole selves to the Reality we call God. This relationship is never complete in this life, for we know ourselves only incompletely and our view of God is part reality, part fantasy. As with our human relationships, however, communion with God in Christ can become progressively deeper. This is the great spiritual adventure and if, on the way, we lose some of our fears and tensions, and learn how better to cope with others, these are only a part of the enrichment we gain.

'I will give you rest'

CHAPTER 10

'I will give you rest'

Has Christ's offer of rest to the overburdened (Matt. 11:28-30) any relevance in mental pain or neurotic suffering? Perhaps sufficient has already been said to encourage an affirmative answer, yet it is to this important question that we must return in conclusion. For from the beginning we have had the Christian sufferer in mind, not because his emotional difficulties are of a peculiar kind, but because thousands of believers would admit that in neurotic distress their Christian profession was merely an added burden. Their problems have been so misunderstood by their fellow-Christians, and sometimes by those who should have been their spiritual guides, that the only thing their religion seemed to contribute to the situation was increased guilt.

By personal experience and through sharing people's problems some of us have been made so sensitive to the distress caused by the preaching that claims too much that we may be in danger of claiming too little. Or perhaps it is rather that we all—the too-brash purveyors of easy solutions and the too-hesitant doubters of whether there are solutions—fail to recognise the real miracle of God's grace. We naturally want to remove suffering and restore, as soon as possible to the disturbed mind, the psychological *status quo*. God, it would seem, is more ambitious and can wait an intolerably long time to achieve His goals.

Christian biography certainly gives us no ground for believing that religious faith and practice necessarily, or immediately, resolves the kind of problems we have considered in this book. Some of the greatest saints have endured prolonged mental pain. Francis of Assisi, usually thought of as one of the sunniest and most tranquil of God's servants, passed through periods of intense depression and desolation.

What can we hope for, then, from our religious faith? How can Christ's claim be validated for those whose burden takes this particular form?

* * *

Many sufferers have witnessed to a spiritual alchemy whereby pain has been transmuted, riches wrested from what seemed sheer waste. For instance, Rosalind Chalmers was a polio victim and spent many months in hospital. She movingly describes her feelings on the first occasion when she was brought down from her upstairs ward and viewed the hospital lawn at close quarters again. 'We stopped, and I stared at it in astonishment and exaltation. Its greenness was of a quality beyond memory and beyond imagination. I drank it in, and it was as if my body had lacked some mysterious chlorophyll of its own which it now recognised and absorbed. That moment should be put in the scales against all the previous pain and frustration and humiliation; *and I think the scales would balance.*'

How comforting if we could assert that in all suffering this possibility is present! But the person enduring mental pain will not be slow to point out that whereas physical disablement often leaves the central personality comparatively unscathed, this is not true of emotional illness. In this suffering the very citadel of the human spirit is overwhelmed. In acute depression and anxiety, in the grip of a phobia or obsessed with deviant desires, a person's freedom of choice is minimal. Only those who have suffered so, or come very close to the victims of these disorders, realise the extent of this.

Fortunately, neurotic suffering is rarely uninterrupted by brighter spells when troublesome symptoms recede. Indeed it often happens that after months or several years of strain and difficulty people emerge completely from their distress. It is often what we do with our suffering in between the periods of intense unhappiness, or after it is over, that can bring untold gain from what seems total loss. Will we then turn our back upon the pain, almost deny its existence, keep well away from those who might, through their own distress, remind us of the abyss still not far away? Certainly there are some who act in this way and perhaps their anxiety leaves them no alternative.

It is also possible, however, to bring away from our own encounter with darkness a depth of sympathy, a compassion for human weakness, and an insight into the complexities of our own nature which add up to a very positive contribution. William James, one of the pioneer psychologists, suffered from a lifelong neurosis and periodically wrestled with the demons of despair. Yet he achieved enough objectivity to observe his own reactions and add to the sum of human knowledge thereby. His own ills remained uncured but they were not unused.

Because faith in Christ helps the believer to see his life in the broader dimension of God's purpose, he is encouraged to look for ways in which his personal distress might be used for the greater good of others. The French proverb, 'Suffering passes; having suffered never passes', is as true of mental pain as of any other distress. And this realisation that some good can be wrested from the darkest experience does have, in some strange way, a healing element.

Can we, however, expect more from our faith in Christ than the grace to turn our problems to constructive use in terms of greater sympathy and understanding of others? I believe we can.

In his contribution to the book of essays *Psychoanalysis Observed*, Anthony Storr writes, 'It seems probable that there are two main factors which promote a person's recovery from the kind of neurotic distress which we have been considering. Both enter into psychoanalysis but neither are peculiar to it; and each factor may operate independently upon patients who are not being analysed but seeking help in other ways. The first factor is that the patient adopts some scheme or system of thought which appears to him to make sense out of his distress. The second is that he makes a relationship of a fruitful kind with another person.'

Let us look at these two factors to see what place they may have in Christian living.

The main difficulty the Christian has of adopting 'some scheme or system of thought which appears to him to make sense of his distress' is that he is often already imprisoned in a moralistic scheme which effectively precludes healing, and in fact aggravates all his problems. He sees his difficulties in terms of guilt and failure and often refuses to look for the deep underlying causes. Indeed, he suspects that looking for causes is a moral evasion, an attempt to excuse his wickedness. Contrary to what some religious people believe, weighing the comparative sinfulness of our actions is a rather superficial activity bearing little fruit in amendment of life. Far greater moral courage is required to look for the cause of our actions, and seek to understand our motivation, than to keep bewailing the fact that we are 'miserable sinners'.

The futility of moralism is a frequent theme in the New Testament. The Pharisees were the most ardent seekers of moral perfection in Christ's day and were also our Lord's bitterest opponents. The letters of Paul continually contrast the burden of living 'under the law' with the freedom of life 'in Christ'.

Often it is only when we have pursued with unflagging zeal the way of moralism right up to the point of emotional and spiritual breakdown that we realise its futility. Why is the moral struggle, pursued in this particular way, so self-defeating?

One reason is that the quest for moral perfection, when undertaken in order to pacify or placate a stern, wrathful deity, or embarked upon in order to raise ourselves above our fellows, is as essentially self-centred as any other human activity. And since true morality, which flows from a loving heart, requires self-forgetfulness, it is as far removed from the tense, anxious piety of the moralist as it could possibly be.

The self-centred nature of the search for self-justification is well documented in Franz Kafka's novel *The Trail*. The hero of the book, Joseph K, is visited one morning at his lodgings by the police who inform him that he is under arrest. The charge is not specified and the police depart without taking Joseph K with them. At first Joseph K ignores the absurd charge but gradually he becomes obsessed with trying to vindicate his innocence. His encounter with the juridical apparatus of the law-courts, advocates, magistrates, judges, is totally frustrating, and the rest of the novel is devoted to his agonised attempts to prove his innocence.

The Trial illustrates how futile is the search for self-justification. What is more it shows how essentially selfish such a quest always is. Joseph K becomes increasingly thoughtless of other people as his obsessive need for self-justification grips him more firmly.

True morality begins, not with a quest for self-vindication, nor yet with a lament that such vindication is impossible; it begins when we respond to a love which raises us out of our self-concern altogether, including our self-esteem. This the gospel of God's love in Christ is able to do.

Another reason why the moralistic scheme of thought, which thinks only in categories of right and wrong, leads to a dead-end is that it provides no place of rest and security outside the self. It demands that we either deceive ourselves into thinking we are good or risk falling into despair. That one or other of these two alternatives is inevitable is proved over and over again by those whose frame of thought is essentially moralistic. It is not too sweeping a judgment to say that they all tend to be either self-righteous, with little insight into their own natures, or burdened by self-hatred.

Paul Tournier describes two ways in which he has tried to help people who are obsessed and humiliated by the vulgarity or the cruelty of their thoughts. The first is to suggest that such ideas are not a true part of their personality since they actually fight and deplore them. Unfortunately, he found that this rarely pacified his patients. He therefore adopted another course by saying to them, 'Of course you have horrible thoughts, because evil is woven into the heart of man, and he is utterly powerless, by himself, to subdue it. This is in fact what the Bible teaches. Everyone has thoughts of which he is ashamed.' Paul Tournier then proceeds to speak to his patients of God's acceptance of us *as we are*. Ultimately the one ground for confidence that we have is in God. And it is only when we have totally surrendered the idea that we can earn God's love that we become free to be objective about ourselves in a way that leads to insight and healing.

I would strongly contend that this moralistic scheme of thought in which some religious people are imprisoned is not even Christian, and that a true understanding of what the New Testament means by the grace of God sets a person free to begin the quest for self-awareness and maturity. In the gospel narratives Jesus is presented as a Man in whose presence the moral failures and outcasts of society felt truly at ease. This could only have been because Christ did not accentuate their guilt but showed them a far more positive road to a new life. The letters of Paul reverberate with the proclamation that God's acceptance of the sinner is not dependent upon his reformation, *but is the moral dynamic which inspires it*.

That God's love precedes anything we may do to be more worthy, and persists in spite of all our failures, is a truth that some of us take years to learn. We suspect that there could be something almost immoral about a love that is unrelated to our worthiness and that is offered to saint and sinner alike. When will we finally grasp the fact that morality which aims at earning love is always stilted, inflexible and brittle? Only morality which is a response to a love that is already there, irrespective of our goodness or badness, is spontaneous and reliable.

Psychiatrists and counsellors who suspect religion of being a pernicious influence in the lives of those they are trying to help do so because they see it as productive of guilt which fixates their patients in the situation of the unfortunate child who believes he must be good or he will lose his parents' affection. This is indeed the way some religious people think of God, but this view is derived from their own pathology, not from the gospels. What the Christian sufferer requires, therefore, is not to be liberated from religion (as some psychiatrists imagine) but to rediscover the religion that is centred upon the life and teaching of Jesus Christ.

To return to the two factors which Anthony Storr suggests promote recovery from neurotic distress, I would claim that the Christian gospel, rightly understood as God's unconditional offer of love and forgiveness, does liberate the sufferer so that he can begin to understand his problems. And when these are insoluble, perhaps because their origins lie beyond recall, the knowledge that he is accepted by God considerably modifies his difficulties. The need of a number of Christians is a rediscovery of what has traditionally been called the doctrine of justification by faith.

But what of the other factor which facilitates healing—the establishing of 'a relationship of a fruitful kind with another person'? It would be easy at this point to claim that the believer's communion with God is all that is required to promote recovery. Indeed there are many for whom this relationship is so real that, once it is freed from neurotic distortions, it does become the vital factor leading to wholeness. So one woman who had come to rest in God's love instead of her own attempts at goodness was able to say, 'Just now I am happy again, because I have entrusted the worst and the best of myself to God, including everything

125

that still resists Him.'

It remains true, however, that some good and earnest people find it all but impossible to *feel* about their relationship to God the same keen and lively reality that marks human relationships. This, as has already been suggested, is surely where the fellowship of the Christian community is important. God's love often becomes real for us through the love of our fellows and it is the task of the church, not only to mediate God's love to the world, but to provide for its own members 'an accepting community'. The phrase that the apostle Paul so frequently used to describe the Christian life—'in Christ'—had a twofold implication. It denoted the intimacy of the believer's communion with his Lord; it also spoke of his incorporation in the Christian fellowship.

Too often it is precisely in this Christian fellowship that men have expected to be judged, condemned and criticised for their faults. When it has been true to its own origins and purpose, however, the church provides that healing and kindly support that everyone needs.

I could end this book in no other way than by affirming my faith that the words of Christ—'I will give you rest'—do hold true for those who wrestle with 'rebel emotions' and suffer mental pain. Trust in Christ does not resolve every problem but it is significant that during His earthly life Jesus was regarded as a great healer as well as a teacher. And many whom respectable society regarded as misfits found newness of life in following Jesus. In His presence men and women learnt to be compassionate towards themselves as well as towards others. They came to value their own individuality because He valued them so highly. They found in Him the very reverse of that condemning rejection offered by the Pharisees. In as far as His love becomes a reality in our lives, both by prayer and in the community of those who seek to follow Him, we are strengthened to step out courageously upon the road to self-knowledge and wholeness. And

126

although this road winds tortuously at times, and even appears to turn back upon itself so that we seem to return again and again to the same place, patient plodding does result in progress. This progress is not at first, and may never be, the disappearance of all neurotic symptoms; it is marked by that greater self-acceptance which leads also to the understanding acceptance of our neighbour.